Their *Faith* Has *Touched* Us

Their *Faith* Has *Touched* Us

The Legacies of Three Young Oklahoma City Bombing Victims

María Ruiz Scaperlanda

Foreword by
Oklahoma City Archbishop Eusebius J. Beltran

Afterword by
Oklahoma Governor Frank Keating
and First Lady Cathy Keating

Cover Photographs:
Mark Bolte (top); Valerie Koelsch (middle), Julie Welch (bottom)

Sheed & Ward™ is a service of The National Catholic Reporter Publishing Company.

Library of Congress Cataloguing-in-Publication Data:
Scaperlanda, María Ruiz, 1960-
    Their faith has touched us : the legacies of three young Oklahoma City bombing victims / María Ruiz Scaperlanda.
        p.   cm.
    ISBN 1-58051-023-X (alk. paper)
    1. Bolte, Mark, 1966-1995. 2. Koelsch, Valerie, 1962-1995.
3. Welch, Julie, 1971-1995. 4. Catholics--Oklahoma--Oklahoma City--Biography. 5. Victims of terrorism--Oklahoma--Oklahoma City--Biography. 6. Oklahoma City Federal Building Bombing, Oklahoma City, Ok la., 1995. I. Title.
BX4651.2.S3 1991
248.4'82--dc21   97-44522
                                                                CIP

Published by: Sheed & Ward
                115 E. Armour Blvd.
                P.O. Box 419492
                Kansas City, MO 64141-6492

To order, call: (800) 333-7373

Cover design by Biner Design.

www.natcath.com/sheedward

This book is reprinted on recycled paper.

To Joyce and Don Bolte,
Rosemary and Harry Koelsch,
Lena Welch, and Bud Welch,
who opened to the rest of the world
the beauty of their children

Contents

Acknowledgments

IT HAS BEEN AN HONOR to come to know Mark Bolte, Valerie Koelsch, and Julie Welch through the eyes of those who knew them. Their stories have inspired me, moved me, and challenged me in my daily walk with Jesus.

This project could not have been possible without the selfless giving of Joyce and Don Bolte, Rosemary and Harry Koelsch, Lena Welch, and Bud Welch. Their willingness to open their hearts and homes has been a gift to me and, through this book, to the rest of the world. I know because of their sharing they allowed themselves to feel a deeper level of pain. I pray that it has also allowed for a further level of healing.

I am also indebted to the countless relatives and friends of Mark, Valerie, and Julie who took the time to share with me—through letters, phone conversations, and meetings— their stories of these three beautiful Catholic Christians. Their sharing became the heart of this book. Special thanks to Archbishop Eusebius J. Beltran and Governor Frank Keating and First Lady Cathy Keating for taking the time to contribute a foreword and an afterword for the book. I am grateful to

Archbishop Beltran for the opportunity to work on this extraordinary project.

I am especially thankful to my husband and partner, Michael, for carrying the extra load and for energizing me through his love; and to my children—Christopher, Anamaría, Rebekah, and Michelle—for the patience, love, and support that enabled me to work on this project.

Finally, I pray that these stories will bless you as they have been a blessing to me.

Peace and all good,

María Ruiz Scaperlanda
August 20, 1997
Feast of St. Bernard, doctor of the Church

Foreword

By Oklahoma City Archbishop
Eusebius J. Beltran

As I was driving to Saint Patrick Church in Oklahoma City, I felt great apprehension despite the fact that it was a bright and beautiful spring day in 1995. By the time I arrived there, not only had the weather changed but the same tension I experienced within me seemed now to hover over the large crowd that had gathered. We had come together for the funeral of Valerie Koelsch. All of us, citizens of Oklahoma City, were still reeling from the April 19 bombing of the Murrah Building. We were not only shocked by the large number of deaths but were also very personally affected. In that horrible number there were individuals like Valerie Koelsch whom we knew and loved, with whom we lived and worked, with whom we hoped and prayed.

Although Saint Patrick seats five hundred people and can accommodate many more in its unique courtyard just outside the clear glass walls of the Church, it was not at all large enough that day to hold the great numbers who had come but could not get in. As I worked my way through the crowd before and after

Mass, I was amazed by the great number of young adults, contemporaries of Valerie who had gathered for the final farewell.

I recalled a similar scene a few days earlier when crowds of young people overflowed the Church of the Epiphany and Resurrection Cemetery for the funeral of Julie Welch. The many young people present there were not only a tribute to Julie but at the same time a tribute to her Catholic faith. The many printed stories and testimonies that began to appear in the *Sooner Catholic* as well as the *Daily Oklahoman* confirmed this fact—that these two young women had indeed been witnesses of our faith.

Shortly after the funerals of Valerie and Julie, I received a copy of the *Arkansas Catholic* and read a similar account about young Mark Bolte. Mark, like Valerie and Julie, had also died in the Murrah Building bombing. Like Valerie and Julie, Mark, too, was a witness to the beauty, the truth, and the goals of our Catholic faith.

Jesus said: "Let your light shine before people so that seeing your good works, they may give praise to your Father in heaven" (Matthew 5:16).

The light of living faith, practiced so fervently in each of these young people, did indeed shine out. These young people were believing, practicing Catholics. They were great witnesses. They believed in Jesus and now we believe that even though they have died, they will live forever with Jesus, our Life and our Resurrection.

The days and weeks immediately after the bombing of the Murrah Building were a trying time for all of us in Oklahoma City. Yet it was also a time of somber reflection on the real meaning and value and goal of human life. Thus I began to marvel at the testimony Valerie, Julie, and Mark had given in their lives, their deaths, and above all in the practice of their Catholic faith. I thought of the many other young people in Oklahoma and beyond, growing up in a world of conflicts and contradictions, and know that they too can profit from the examples of Valerie, Julie, and Mark.

As we approach the end of this millennium, we are startled by the violence, injustice, and confusion so prevalent in our society. Fortunately we know that this is not universal. There are indeed many good and faithful people, young and old, rich and poor, men and women who reflect the goodness of God in their daily lives. Accordingly, we recognize the example these three young people gave as evidence of the living faith that will overcome the darkness.

In asking María Ruiz Scaperlanda to write this book, it was my intention to make known to our young people the value and the beauty of our Catholic faith through the example and testimony of Valerie, Julie, and Mark. I believe this purpose has been well fulfilled. The testimonies of so many people about the witness of Valerie, Julie, and Mark should be a great incentive and inspiration for all our young people. It is a lesson that young people need to learn in order to better understand who they are, why they are here, and how they should live.

María Ruiz Scaperlanda has effectively compiled these testimonies and weaves them in the context of the prayer of Saint Francis of Assisi "Make Me an Instrument of Your Peace." Now, I challenge all young people to read these, think about them, and apply them to your daily lives.

Valerie, Julie, and Mark were three fun-loving young Catholics who cherished and lived their faith. May all who read this book come closer to God in their daily lives.

Most Reverend Eusebius J. Beltran
Archbishop of Oklahoma City
July 1997

Introduction

Remembering April 19, 1995

As a horror-stricken world watched on their television screens the bloody images from the worst terrorist act in United States history, those who live in the country's Heartland held their breath. The lives of thousands of residents in Central Oklahoma were left hanging, like the dust in the air. No one in this midwestern capital city spoke of anything else, no one thought of anything else—and everyone seemed to know somebody affected by the April 19, 1995, bombing of the Alfred P. Murrah Federal Building.

When I first arrived at the site of the Murrah Building to report on the disaster for Catholic News Service, police lines had already been drawn and emergency crews had created makeshift shelters and arranged work sites. In a matter of hours, budding spring gardens succumbed to a field full of military tents, hastily erected to serve as a temporary morgue, as ATF/FBI evidence gathering sites, and as a canteen for rescue workers. Law enforcement and military personnel—all fully armed—lined the streets, carefully eyeing every approaching person and vehicle. A breathing mask, pieces of bloodied bandage, and much broken glass—hastily swept to the edge in an attempt to clear the sidewalks—silently testified to the human carnage that had taken place there hours before. Overhead, a helicopter circled the downtown radius accusingly pointing a flood light at the empty streets. The sounds of sirens, voices, and motors blended effectively with the humming of drilling equipment just a few blocks away, where workers used flood lights and cranes to continue rescue operations around the clock.

What the women and men, working in rescue teams of a hundred at a time, experienced at the bomb site will inevitably haunt them for the rest of their lives: pieces of debris, twisted metal, and shards of broken glass blended with the smell of death and reminders of those who worked here—purses, pieces of clothing, toys, shoes, and grisly body parts. "It's worse than the most horrible Friday the 13th movie you can imagine—you can't walk out of this theater," said twenty-five-year-old Steve Mavros from the Oklahoma Canine Search and Rescue out of Tulsa. Mavros, who had been deployed to the site with his specially trained dog, Bucephalos, to identify the location of humans and human remains, said this was the first mission for several in their ten-dog team. "We would have a hit—a human find—but only find a piece of a body. I feel pity for the people who've been cut to ribbons, trapped alive in the metal and concrete. I feel shock, disgust, and more sorrow than I can describe." At the site that was once the Murrah Building, a mass grave opened up into what became known as "the pit." From the open offices above, papers from tattered file cabinets flew continuously into the streets below carried along by the never-ending Oklahoma wind. A lone suit coat still hung several stories high from what was once the back wall of the building, testimony to the hundreds of lives that had once worked here.

Northwest of the site, a block-long square area had instantaneously become an international media center amidst fallen debris, van food vendors, and demolished cars. It became known as Satellite City. Reporters talked on cell phones to frantic editors, photographers pointed their high-powered telephoto lenses at rescue operations on the site, and television crews in mobile homes staked their on-the-spot area for the next broadcast. Volunteer organizations promptly brought in truckloads of food and clothes for rescue personnel—some of whom arrived in Oklahoma City from around the country with only the clothes on their backs to relieve the already exhausted Oklahoma workers. The entire downtown area, limited to a few access entry points from the outlining interstate highways, seemed to be under martial law.

Over time, Oklahoma City has confronted its injuries, revealing scars that run much deeper than the 220 buildings; piping, waterway, and electrical systems; and hundreds of cars in the downtown area affected by the blast. Along with the ruins and the changed skyline, Oklahoma City has also heard courageous and inspiring tales of those who lived and those who died; of strangers becoming family as rescuers searched for hope in what remained of this once nine-story building.

The world knows that 168 people died (171 counting the unborn) and hundreds of others were maimed and injured in the blast that ripped through the cool air that spring morning. And, while it is difficult to use the word *blessing* amidst such a painful healing process, the stories of faith in this city community are also ingrained in America's memory: stories of devoted volunteers, of tireless rescue workers who risked their lives in the still-trembling building, of still-hopeful survivors, and of faithful victims' families. These are the stories that continue to heal the city's and the country's wounds. As Tom Brokaw said of his week-long experience covering the terrorist act, "Oklahomans may feel more vulnerable now, a little disoriented by what's happened to them, but in their response to this madness, they have elevated us all with their essential sense of goodness, community, and compassion."

Many stories testify to the honesty of this town of five hundred thousand. There was no looting in this wrecked downtown. In fact, members still talk about how when the open vault of the Federal Employees Credit Union was blown apart by the bomb blast, thousands of dollar bills blew up into the air and floated down into the chaotic streets. What's extraordinary about that story is that for days following the blast, money was turned in. And when all the money was gathered and counted, the Credit Union ended up with more money than originally held in the vault. Even the city's crime rate went down for several days.

There isn't much left at the fateful downtown site. A piece of the base of the Murrah Building remains. Grass now covers the epicenter of the blast and its surroundings. The bombing site and the chain-link fence that encircles it have become a shrine, with visitors continuing to make daily pilgrimages to this place of inexplicable destruction. Spontaneously, new and returning visitors stand in reverent silence at the fence. This is truly a holy place. Those who come to the fence hope to touch the untouchable. They leave ribbons, pictures, signed articles, flags, live and artificial flowers, teddy bears, and hand-scribbled messages of hope on cardboard and paper. Some have even taken the shirt off their back, literally, and somehow attached it to the fence with their personal message. Americans and visitors from all over the world continue to come to this impromptu Fifth Street memorial to mourn, to cry, to pray, and to remember. And plans have been approved for a permanent memorial in downtown Oklahoma City.

It is *important* for the United States community to remember those who died in Oklahoma City on April 19, 1995, but it is *essential* to remember how they lived. This book celebrates the lives of three young citizens, ordinary people who lived their faith in extraordinary ways and who died together at the Alfred P. Murrah Building.

Although they never met each other, Mark Bolte, Valerie Koelsch, and Julie Welch shared several parallels in their lives. All three were single young adults who integrated their faith into every sphere of their lives: family, church, school, work, and friendships. They were federal employees, although serving in different agencies, who believed that their work—and how they performed it—made a difference in our world. Those who knew Mark, Valerie, and Julie want them to be remembered not for the fact that they all died at 9:02 on that April 19, but for the faith and love by which they lived. Their stories tell of lives distinguished by devotion, love, dedication, friendship, loyalty, commitment, and faithfulness.

The family, friends, and co-workers who remember Mark, Valerie, and Julie hope that, through their memories, others will come to know their friends and loved ones. But perhaps more importantly, they desire that those who hear their stories may come to see the importance of living life to the fullest—and to honor the source of that life. Mark, Valerie, and Julie honored God by how they lived, and they drew on the deep roots of their Catholic faith as a source of their strength. By celebrating their lives, without ignoring their deaths, the stories of Mark, Valerie, and Julie become the flowers that will bloom in the ashes.

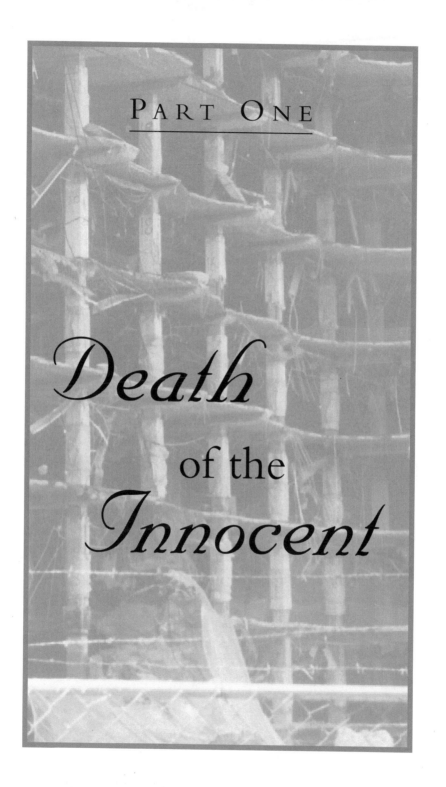

PART ONE

Death
of the
Innocent

Chapter 1

The
Faith Legacies of
Mark Bolte,
Valerie Koelsch,
and
Julie Welch

Mark Bolte

MARK ALLEN BOLTE, twenty-eight, was an environmental engineer at the Federal Highway Administration. At 6' 4" and 250 pounds, strawberry-blonde Mark was known at work and church as a big guy with a heart full of love for his family; his friends; and the Arkansas Razorbacks, the university he graduated from in 1990. Mark, who had only moved to Oklahoma in January, is described as both "a great big teddy bear" and "the boy next door" by his friends and co-workers.

Mark was born October 21, 1966, in Bentonville, Arkansas, to Joyce Mount and Don Bolte. Joyce, who was born in Lamar, Colorado, claims Arkansas as her home. Don was born in Tomahawk, Wisconsin. The Boltes met, made a home, and raised their two boys, Mark and Matt, in Bentonville. Mark graduated from Bentonville High School in 1985 with honors and four years of perfect attendance. He was a member of the Chess Club and the Future Business Leaders of America. Mark attended Arkansas Tech University in Russellville for three years and transferred to the University of Arkansas where he received a bachelor's degree in civil engineering. He was a member of the American Society of Civil Engineers and of the Lambda Chi Alpha Fraternity.

Although his work with the United States Department of Transportation's Federal Highway Administration took Mark all over the country—stationing him in North

Carolina, Oregon, Colorado, Vermont, and Texas before his transfer to Oklahoma City—Mark's easy smile made him someone who generated friends quickly. Mark loved Denver, Colorado, specifically and told his parents that he'd welcome the chance to go back there to work. His first job after training, however, was in Austin, Texas, an assignment he held until January of 1995 when he transferred to Oklahoma City. "Mark was good with new folks in the office," remarked co-worker Amy Heflin, who was transferred to the Austin division office from Boston about a year after Mark arrived. "He wanted to show you around the office and invite you over for dinner." Mark had a chance to stay in Austin but decided to move to Oklahoma City to pursue environmental engineering, his dream job.

Oklahoma City co-worker Becky Lawson remembers Mark's wonderful sense of humor, even when being teased. "The women in the office teased him a lot about just getting out of bed because no matter what he did, his hair was always messed up!" she laughs. "Even in the short time I knew him, I was very impressed by Mark, his demeanor, his attitude about life. He was so outgoing and friendly; it's easy to see how he would have a very positive effect on others." Co-worker Theodore Miller remembers Mark's spirit at Christmas. His final Christmas in Austin, Miller notes, Mark made a point of going through the office and giving everyone a small candy cane as he wished each person a Merry Christmas.

"He had a knack for telling if something was wrong (with a person)," remembers his mother, Joyce Bolte. "We all know he's watching over somebody, even now." Mark loved to make people smile, and he let his attitude lead the way. He loved to surprise his family and friends with cards, for any occasion and for no occasion. His friends remember Mark playing basketball and the way he reached what they called "the giggle zone," a way of making sure everyone, no matter how competitive, had a good time while they played. Mark's hobby was model airplanes, which he hung everywhere in his room. His brother, Matt, now has many of Mark's models hanging in his own bedroom. Mark was known as a walking sports encyclopedia. He played basketball, golf, and had recently taken up rollerblading. He also played the guitar and was very artistic. His talent showing itself in doodles on scrap paper during meetings. Mark loved to watch hockey, the Atlanta Braves, and Joe Montana. Shortly before his death, Mark traveled to Dallas to see the Stars hockey game with friends from the Austin office.

When Mark left Austin for Oklahoma City, his Texas co-workers said to his future boss: "You're getting a great big teddy bear." Mark's loving attitude gave him a special touch with younger people, and many co-workers treasure Mark's gift as a young adult role model for their children. "Mark exemplified the meaning of Eagle Scout. He volunteered to be an adult leader for Oklahoma City's Troop 177 and was an instant hit with the boys," remembers co-worker Bruce Lind. "Mark had a profound impact on the boys and the adult leaders of Troop 177. When the troop replaced its old troop flag, the new one was dedicated to his memory." In his hometown of Bentonville, Arkansas, and at his family's church in neighboring Rogers, Mark is still remembered as a devoted Eagle Scout and a Knight of the Altar. In his senior year, Mark was named Knight of the Year by the other altar servers. Every year after moving away Mark returned to serve at midnight Mass, as is the tradition for altar server alumni at Saint Vincent de Paul Church in Rogers. That final Christmas he served alongside his younger brother, Matt. At Mark's funeral Mass, dozens of altar servers flanked the Saint Vincent de Paul Church entrance and main aisle, serving as an honor guard. The church overflowed with those paying last respects.

The last time the Boltes saw Mark was on Easter Sunday. He attended Mass with his family at Saint Vincent de Paul's and spent the afternoon at home in Bentonville. He left for Oklahoma that afternoon, stopping at his Aunt Retha's home in Tahlequah, Oklahoma, on the way. That night he called to let his parents know that he had arrived safely. Three days later, the Bolte's received a phone call confirming that Mark had been in the Murrah Building at the time of the explosion. Don, Joyce, and Matt headed to Oklahoma City that night and, for what seemed like an eternity, waited to hear news about their son. Since Mark had only moved to the city a few months before, that trip was the parents' first visit to Mark's new apartment. Matt had visited his brother in Oklahoma City once before.

Mark was the last Federal Highway Administration employee pulled from the rubble—and one of the last few retrieved. The days were long and weary for his waiting family. Occupying themselves between the morning and afternoon briefings became a real challenge. After waiting fifteen days for the news, Mark's body was recovered on Thursday, May 4, a few hours before the official search was called off. "We thought we were going to have to come home without him," remembers Joyce Bolte.

As long as there was a remote chance that Mark was alive, Joyce, Don, and Matt avoided cleaning out Mark's apartment. "When we were told that the possibilities were getting less and less likely that anybody was alive, Matt and I started packing," remembers Don. "It was hard. We probably spent as much time looking at stuff as we did packing." Among the things found by Mark's parents in his apartment was a well-worn Bible with two bookmarks. One was in the book of Judges, the other was at the beginning of the Gospel of Mark.

The Boltes are filled with gratitude for the numerous acts of kindness they experienced those two weeks living in Oklahoma City. The Wal-Mart home office, where Joyce works back in Bentonville, supplied a U-Haul truck and driver to transport Mark's household goods and furnishings home. The company also supplied angels to the Red Cross Emergency Center at First Christian Church in Oklahoma City, where family members spent their days decorating them and waiting for the bodies to be identified. Employees of an Oklahoma City Wal-Mart store brought food to the Boltes daily at the apartment. Friends from Northwest Arkansas drove to Oklahoma City to be with them. And two priests, Father Lowell L. Stieferman and Father David F. Monahan, visited them at Mark's apartment.

On the morning of April 19, Mark and his co-workers assembled together for a 9:00 A.M. round-table conference meeting on the fourth floor of the Murrah Building. Mark was one of eleven Federal Highway Administration employees killed that morning.

Valerie Koelsch

VALERIE JO KOELSCH boasted of having three families—her God-given family into which she was born, her church family with whom she shared a deep faith in God, and her

Federal Employees Credit Union family with whom she enjoyed being each day.

Valerie was born March 5, 1962, in Oklahoma City. She attended Saint Patrick's Elementary, Putnam City Schools, and Saint Gregory's College before graduating from Oklahoma State University, Stillwater, with a degree in Business Administration and Business Management. As marketing director for the Federal Employees Credit Union, Valerie, thirty-three, was responsible for all marketing activities, including promotion, staff training, product development, public relations, and market research. Co-workers remember Valerie as someone who did her job well, twice winning CUNA's Bridge Award for Excellence in Newsletter Communication for FECU's newsletter, the "Silver Eagle Gazette." She was also awarded the Dora Maxwell Award for Social Responsibility. At OSU, Valerie earned the Dean's Honor Roll and was selected as one of thirteen Outstanding Marketing Major Seniors by the Marketing Faculty. She worked at the Credit Union for eleven years—from the time she graduated from OSU in 1984. Through her work at the Credit Union, Valerie traveled and made friends all over the United States. She had a reputation for being a "lover of life," always smiling and joking.

Valerie came from deep Oklahoma roots and a strong union family. Her ancestors came to Oklahoma during the early 1900s, before Oklahoma statehood. Her grandfather was a member of the Sheet Metal Workers Union Local 124 for over thirty-eight years. Her father, Harry, a life-long member of Local 124, also served as president of the union. He also served as chairman of the board of the Oklahoma City IBEW (International Brotherhood of Electrical Workers) Federal Credit Union. Like her father, Val was dedicated to the credit union movement. Her mother, Rosemary, is a member of the Oklahoma Education Association, and her brother is a business representative for the Operating Engineers Local 627.

Valerie's parents, Harry Jo Koelsch and Rosemary Schachle, both natives of Oklahoma City, attended Saint Joseph's Catholic School, which was located at the same site where the Murrah Building was later erected. "We've said that it's kind of holy ground down there," says Harry Koelsch. "We went to school in that same spot that became our daughter's tomb." Harry and Rosemary also both graduated from Mount Saint Mary High School, where they met when alumnus Harry came back for a high school football game. The Koelschs are active parishioners at Saint Patrick Catholic Church. Rosemary's parents, Joe and Urilla Schachle, were founding members of Saint Patrick's.

Valerie, too, became a member of Saint Patrick Church, where she helped launch its Young Adult Ministry, served on its parish council, was a Eucharistic Minister, a member of the parish softball team, and participated in its Young Adult Core Team. Valerie also served as a member of the archdiocesan Young Adult Core Team. "Something in her made everyone want to know her," said Valerie Mitchell, then-associate director of Youth and Young Adult Ministry for the Archdiocese of Oklahoma City. "She had this great smile—and a quiet, almost dry sense of humor. She had these zingers—she almost read your mind and called you on it."

In 1993, Valerie led a group from the Archdiocese of Oklahoma City to Denver for World Youth Day, an experience that affected her deeply. "Valerie was committed to

Young Adult Ministry and proud of her Catholic faith," remembers her friend Kristi Mohr, who made the trip with Valerie. "And she wanted others to experience the Church and its people. She experienced and helped others experience the family that the Catholic Church is—a family that is worldwide. She demonstrated well Jesus' teaching on discipleship that the greatest among you will be the servant."

Valerie often made time for her family and friends, taking time off from work when needed. Attorney Wm. G. Newhouse remembers the numerous times that Val provided transportation for her grandmother so that she could come to his office. "It is obvious that she was a loving, caring person. The few discussions I had with her let me know that she was all a person could hope for in a granddaughter, friend, and co-worker." Val was often found spending time with her brothers, Terry and Gregory, and her sister, Michelle. She loved children and was deeply involved in the lives of her nieces and nephew. On Holy Saturday, just four days before her death, Valerie accompanied her parents to Arlington, Texas, to be with her brother, Terry, and his wife, Rhonda, to celebrate the third birthday of her niece, Kayla. To add to the celebration, Kayla's little sister was born that same day. While Kayla's parents were at the hospital, Val and Rosemary hosted Kayla's birthday party at McDonald's. The last pictures taken of Valerie were taken on Easter Sunday. They show the proud aunt holding her newborn niece, Taylor Koelsch, born on Holy Saturday.

In the last five days before her death, in fact, Val had the opportunity to see and visit with all of her immediate family members. When Val and her father left Arlington on Easter Sunday, they visited with her other brother, Greg, and his wife, Stephanie, and their daughter, Lindsay—who was at

Baptist Hospital in Oklahoma City recovering from an asthma attack. On Tuesday, April 18, Valerie left the Federal Building for the afternoon to attend a meeting in Tulsa. She did not discover, however, until she arrived, that the meeting had been canceled. Because of the change in plans, Val took the time to visit a good friend who worked in the building where her meeting had been scheduled. Then she headed back to Oklahoma City and stopped in Edmond to visit her younger sister, Michelle, and her husband, Gary, and their son, Austin. Because her meeting was canceled, Val got to spend extra time playing with Austin, who will always treasure the Easter toy that his Aunt Val brought him.

An avid fan of her alma mater, Oklahoma State University, known as the Cowboys, Val had plans to go to Stillwater to watch OSU baseball the third weekend in April. She never made it. Valerie followed football and basketball and played countless hours on many coed softball teams. In spite of being born with a serious foot problem and having multiple foot surgeries and casts as an infant, she had played softball since elementary school. As she did with other obstacles in her life, Valerie did not allow those casts on her feet to limit her.

For Valerie, life was to be lived intensely, and her love of sports provides a powerful metaphor for her view of life. Valerie knew life was a gift from God to be honored and treasured. She was not afraid to get in there and fight the good fight. Her enthusiasm for life drew many to her, and she was claimed by many as their "best friend." Valerie's funeral at Saint Patrick's was attended by approximately fifteen hundred mourners, where friends and family alike remembered her smile and contagious laughter. At Immaculate Conception cemetery, Valerie Jo's headstone shows a portrait of Valerie, topped with a rose-festooned heart. Next to it the inscription reads, "Your spirit will always comfort us, our love for you will last forever, we'll remember you for who you were, our darling, our very special one."

On the morning of April 19, Florence Rogers, the chief executive of FECU, called seven top managers to a meeting in her third-floor office. Valerie's office was located on the west side of the Credit Union, but the meeting put her in the part of the building hardest hit by the bomb. Note pads and coffee mugs in hand, Val and her co-workers sat in couches and chairs around Rogers's desk, Val sitting immediately next to her boss. The explosion collapsed the floor in front of Rogers's desk, and sent the officers—all women—plunging three stories down. Only Rogers survived.

Julie Welch

A SPANISH TRANSLATOR and claims representative for the Social Security Administration, twenty-three-year-old Julie Marie Welch was the only child of Lena M. Compassi of Muskogee, Oklahoma, and Emmett E. "Bud" Welch of Shawnee, Oklahoma. Julie had a step brother named Christopher and a half-brother named Kevin. In her large extended family and her community of friends, Julie was known as a quiet, friendly person with a strong desire to help others.

Julie, born September 12, 1971, grew up in Oklahoma City, attending Windsor Elementary, Wiley Post Elementary, Hefner Junior High, and Bishop McGuinness Catholic High School. "Julie had a level of maturity that allowed her to develop a good rapport with not only her peers, but also her teachers," notes McGuinness Guidance Counselor Mary Jane Rapp. "Julie is one of the few students that I am aware of who was willing to delay her graduation a year in order to attend school in Spain her junior year. I was most impressed with her desire to seek new challenges, her adventurous spirit, and her ability to work toward the accomplishment of her goals. She was definitely a young lady who was not afraid to stretch herself toward high goals." During high school, Julie volunteered at a downtown Hispanic center, explaining utility bills and job application forms to immigrants.

Norma Welch Burton, Julie's aunt from Oklahoma City, recalls how, in junior high school, Julie befriended a new Spanish-speaking classmate who spoke limited English, helping the girl navigate the cafeteria line and standing up for her when others called her derogatory names. It was a life-changing experience for Julie. "She was a genuine, unpretentious, gentle, and loving person who liked to reach out to help others," Burton remembers. Julie not only spent a high school year in Pontevedra, Spain, through Youth for Understanding International Exchange, she also returned to Madrid the spring of her college sophomore year as a part of the Marquette in Madrid program. Julie majored in Spanish at Marquette University in Milwaukee, receiving a Spanish scholarship for each of the four years she attended the university. During her years living in Milwaukee, Julie both participated in and organized activities that reflected her growing concern for social issues. She was a weekly volunteer with the Saint Vincent de Paul Meal Program in Milwaukee, delivering meals to needy families. Their adjunct program to delivering meals—the Family Friendship Program—allowed Julie an opportunity to use her fluency in Spanish to interact with Hispanic children in a mentoring capacity. Julie also volunteered with Milwaukee's Habitat for Humanity program, helping to build homes for needy people. During the Gulf War, Julie organized a prayer service for peace at the university.

Julie was deeply affected by a "Third World Retreat" she attended in the Dominican Republic as a Milwaukee Saint Vincent de Paul student representative. After living for three weeks with a family in a hut with dirt floors and no running water, she cried reflecting on the contrast to her "easy" American life. Julie loved politics, but working with the poor was an even greater love. During spring and summer of 1994, her final year in college, Julie lived at Petawa Residence, a residence for women affiliated with Opus Dei. It was the last two years of her life that Julie's faith—which had been rooted in a desire to better God's world and His people—began to bloom.

Back in Oklahoma City after graduation, Julie was a member of Epiphany of the Lord Catholic Church. "She was a very religious girl," notes Epiphany pastor Rev. Lowell L. Stieferman. "A very gentle person, extremely reverent. She had a very pleasing personality. I remember her and her mom always being together." Julie also attended a weekly young adult prayer meeting at Tinker Air Force Base, where she met Lieutenant Eric Hilz, who became her best friend and fiancee.

She dreamt of becoming a teacher someday and starting a program for Hispanic children in the neighborhood of Little Flower Church where she often attended Mass after work. Julie had planned to leave her job at the Social Security Administration in August to accept a job teaching Spanish. After the bombing, several other schools called, unaware of her death.

Julie's faith was evident at work in how she related to her co-workers as well as how well she performed her job. In her Social Security Performance Evaluation, her reviewer noted, "Julie is very courteous and she projects a genuinely concerned and helpful attitude (in her claims interviews). Julie is a fast learner and shows the ability to learn from her mistakes . . . she demonstrated a keen eye for detail and identification of case discrepancies." Social Security Assistant Manager Dennis Purifoy, says of Julie's work, "Her caring attitude was very evident. I remember her ready smile and what a sweet personality she had. She was on the way to becoming an excellent public servant. I knew this because she was frustrated at not mastering the job quickly (no one can do that). Julie had studied hard to get to where she was, and she was willing to keep on working hard to achieve what she wanted."

Julie gave up a job offer in Chicago after graduation to come home to Oklahoma, telling her friends that her mom, dad, and both grandmothers needed her. She loved to spend time with her extended family and enjoyed surprising them with a visit, a phone call, or a note. Great-uncle Albert Compassi of Muskogee, Oklahoma, explains, "Older family members and young alike enjoyed being around her. She grew into such a lovely young lady. When her grandmother experienced the loss of a limb in 1994, Julie was right there with her mother doing things in the house and checking up on Grandmother." Julie was "very honest, loving, and kind," remembers her uncle, Richard Dominick Compassi of Muskogee. "She was intelligent and generous with her time spent in helping other people." Her aunt, Gloria Welch Murphy of Richardson, Texas, remembers Julie's best quality as being "her humanity and caring for underprivileged people, especially Hispanic children."

Julie believed that understanding would be accomplished through people learning about each other's cultures—and each other's languages. Besides Spanish, she could also converse in Portuguese, Italian, French, and German. As she matured in faith, Julie's compassion for the underprivileged remained a central concern. Her faith offered her hope to face the difficult needs in her life and the world, enabling her to live a life that affected others in a positive way.

Julie developed a special relationship with Saint Thérèse of Lisieux, or Saint Thérèse of the Little Flower. And like Saint Thérèse, Julie concentrated on doing the little things in life, the ordinary things, with love. Many an evening found her encircling Lake Hefner with her mother, Lena, reciting the rosary as the two walked. Her desire to "receive Jesus" in the Eucharist led Julie to a commitment to daily Mass. Julie had even memorized the daily Mass times of churches around the city. Julie and Lena celebrated their last Mass together at Little Flower Church, one of Julie's favorite places, the night before her death. And on April 19, Julie attended 7:00 A.M. Mass at Saint Charles Borromeo Church before going to work at the Federal Building downtown.

About 8:00 A.M. on April 19, 1995, Julie and three other women began straightening files in the stock room of the Social Security office located on the first floor of the Murrah Building. About 9:00 A.M., Julie took her final steps to the front of the Social Security office to meet Emilio Rangel Tapia, a father of five, and the Reverend Gilberto Martinez, the pastor of El Tabernáculo de Fé Church. Tapia, who spoke no English, had an appointment to obtain his Social Security card and Martinez came to help. Julie's three co-workers started to return to the front with her, when a supervisor suggested that they stay in the stockroom until they finished throwing out outdated forms. Julie had left the file area approximately ninety seconds before the bomb went off. Her co-workers in the stockroom survived.

We Will Never Forget

As THE SPECIAL 1996 MEMORIAL ISSUE of the journal *Oklahoma Today* declared: "It is impossible to overstate the significance of the bombing of the Alfred P. Murrah Federal Building in downtown Oklahoma City—to America or to Americans." An Oklahoma City sportscaster faced with the nightly litany of scores several days after the around-the-clock coverage of the disaster, verbalized everybody's feelings when he said, "I'm sorry. I just can't do scores tonight. It just seems meaningless." Words limit the reality of the shock, the terror, and the feelings that still haunt Oklahoma City.

And the profound images of April 1995 will never disappear from the city's memory: panic-stricken men and women running from the blast; children covered with blood being carried out of the rubble; rescuers hugging one another and silently bowing their heads in prayer before leaving the bomb site; television and radio journalists openly sharing their faith on the air; flags tirelessly flying at half mast for months; endless lines of cars with headlights on in the middle of the day; a cross lighting the night sky on all four sides of the Liberty Building downtown; volunteers serving food to weary and teary-eyed firefighters; "Thank you for your work of love" scribbled on a boarded up window near the site; "Pray" silently proclaimed on billboards across the city.

An elm tree still stands facing what was once the Murrah Building. Some of the survivors remember this tree located in the parking lot across from the building as a barometer for those who worked at the Murrah Building. The tree signaled the passing seasons: spring blooms giving way to summer, autumn colors, and the starkness of winter. Julie Welch liked to park her car on the east side of the tree, in the shade, while she was at work. Though ravaged by the power of the bomb, the tree remains, refusing to surrender to violence, vowing to provide fresh buds for many springs to come. Frequent visitors call it the Survivor Tree. Many whose memories are forever etched in the events of that April 19, take heart that the tree remains, a symbol of their own survival.

Prayer for Peace

IN A *DAILY OKLAHOMAN* ARTICLE dated May 27, 1995, Bud Welch and Lena Welch were interviewed at the fence surrounding the site of what was once the Alfred P. Murrah Building. That day, Bud took time to weave a salmon colored rose in the chain link fence near NW Fourth and Robinson, as he and Lena quietly prayed, "Where there is hatred, let me sow love. . . ."

In the aftermath of this tale of destruction, the Prayer for Peace, or Prayer of Saint Francis, serves as a fitting vehicle to present the everyday stories of how three ordinary people lived life in extraordinary ways. The stories that follow are told documentary style and are interwoven with the words from the Prayer for Peace. They are stories collected from interviews and letters and based on information from those who knew Valerie Koelsch, Julie Welch, and Mark Bolte—family members, friends, co-workers, pastors. For each line of the Prayer for Peace, there is a story about Mark, a story about Valerie, and a story about Julie, arranged simply in alphabetical order by last name. The stories vary in length and, because there are many speakers, they also vary in style. They are simple, sometimes funny, and remarkably ordinary. But that is the heart of this story. Mark, Valerie, and Julie changed the world they lived in, not by how they died, but by how they lived.

Pius XI said in the Bull of Canonization for Saint Thérèse of Lisieux that the young French Carmelite nun had, "without going beyond the common order of things in her way of life, followed out and fulfilled her vocation with such alacrity, generosity, and constancy that she reached a heroic degree of virtue." It is an interesting coincidence that this year marks the one hundredth anniversary of Saint Thérèse's death. Mark, Valerie, and Julie were as ordinary as the rest of us. They were dedicated to their work. They liked to play golf and softball. They liked to rollerblade and bike. They loved children. They helped out at the parish and volunteered at the Scout troop. They were also people of prayer who lived out, like Saint Thérèse, a philosophy of "the little way" in the different spheres of their lives. Like the twenty-four-year-old saint from the Carmel at Lisieux, Mark, Valerie, and Julie died young. And perhaps death in their youth makes us uncomfortable. But the fact remains that they, like Saint Thérèse, were a living testimony that "perfection consists in being what God wants us to be." And they showed those of us left behind that this perfection, intricately connected to the small and the ordinary, does not ever require that we achieve great successes—at least, not as the world measures success.

The stories in this book are best experienced slowly, perhaps one at a time, in order to let the simple truths that reside within each one touch the heart of the reader. Words cannot capture the reality of who Mark, Valerie, and Julie were. But they offer us a glimpse into their lives. These stories are meant to be meditations on how an ageless prayer can be lived out in the simple things we do—as Mark, Valerie, and Julie did. They remind us that it's not so much what we do in life that counts, but how we do it. They are meant for each one of us who hope that living our ordinary lives can, indeed, make a difference.

PRAYER FOR PEACE

Lord make me an instrument of your peace
Where there is hatred, let me sow love
Where there is injury, let me sow pardon
Where there is doubt, let me sow faith
Where there is despair, let me sow hope
Where there is darkness, let me sow light
And where there is sadness, let me sow joy.
O Divine Master, grant that I may not so much seek
to be consoled as to console,
To be understood as to understand,
To be loved as to love;
For it is in giving that we receive,
It is in pardoning that we are pardoned,
And it is in dying that we are born to eternal life.

All photos here were taken in April 1995.
A) *25-year-old Steve Mavros, a member of Tulsa's Oklahoma Canine Search and Rescue, and his dog, Bucephalos. Mavros's team was one of dozens from around the country who worked around the clock at the Murrah Building, first as rescue and later as recovery teams.*

B) *Spontaneous signs of hope were seen around the site and the city.* **C)** *First Christian Church in Oklahoma City the day after the bombing. The Red Cross Emergency Center was set up on church grounds as a central source of information for the families of those missing.*

D) *Workers gather in front of an impromptu memorial at the site.* **E)** *Fathers Joseph Meinhart and Joseph Ross, two of many local clergy who ministered to grieving families and rescue workers at the bombing site.*

F) *Oklahoma Governor Frank Keating greets Archbishop Eusebius J. Beltran at the Governor's Mansion on April 23, 1995, the day of the Statewide Prayer Service at the Oklahoma Fair Grounds. Also attending the prayer service, held five days after the bombing, were President Clinton and Evangelist Billy Graham.*

G) *View of the gutted Murrah remains from the building's south side. In the distance is the Journal Record Building, also fatally damaged by the bombing (May 1995).* **H)** *Remains of the Alfred P. Murrah Building in May 1995, days before the building was imploded. Covered with an orange tarp at the site was the area where a lot of bodies were found. It became known as "the pit."* **I)** *A student at St. James Catholic School examines a board made up of some of the hundreds of thousands of letters sent to schools in the Oklahoma City area by people from around the world (May 1995).*

J) *Oklahoma City Archbishop Eusebius J. Beltran processing in for the December 1, 1996, rededication Mass of St. Joseph Old Cathedral, across the street from the Murrah Building. Governor Keating, who is Catholic, stands in the background.* **K)** *Archbishop Beltran celebrates the rededication Mass on December 1.* **L)** *Governor Frank Keating receiving communion from Archbishop Beltran at*

the rededication Mass. **M)** *Oklahoma Governor Frank Keating and Knights of Columbus State Deputy Henry J. Rowe in attendance at the rededication Mass.* **N)** *Rosemary Koelsch (foreground) and Lena Welch present the offertory gifts to Archbishop Beltran at the Oklahoma City bombing second anniversary Mass on April 19, 1997.*

24

All photos here were taken on the day that Timothy McVeigh's verdict was announced, Friday, June 13, 1997. **O)** Family and friends gather underneath the Survivor Tree.
P) Governor Frank Keating and his wife, Cathy, stand under the Survivor Tree along with hundreds of victims' family members and friends. **Q)** Bud Welch, Julie's father, examines a sign on the Survivor Tree. **R)** First Lady Cathy Keating offers words of comfort to Lena Welch, Julie's mother. **S)** Bud Welch is interviewed by someone from the media. He has been very outspoken in both the national and local media (Newsweek, U. S. News, Good Morning America, etc.) regarding his opposition to the death penalty on moral and religious grounds.

25

All photos here were taken in August 1997. **T)** More than two years after the bombing, the Survivor Tree still stands. Because of its location in the parking lot across the street from the Murrah Building and next to the heavily damaged Journal Record Building, survivors and family members see the tree as a sign of hope and a symbol of their own survival. **U)** Grass now covers the site where the two-ton bomb

exploded. Only a wall and some of the main level structure remains of what once was the Murrah Federal Building. The chain link fence surrounding the remains of the building has become a temporary wall of honor. Visitors come daily to the site, leaving behind personal

messages of comfort for the victims and the city. In the background is St. Joseph Old Cathedral, which suffered heavy bomb damage and is now restored.
V) Personal effects left at the Murrah fence include notes, caps, shirts, crosses, flags, teddy bears, and flowers. Plans for a permanent memorial have now been approved.

PART TWO

Instruments

of

Peace

Chapter 2

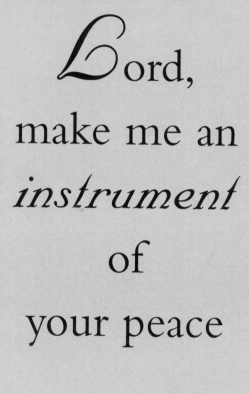

*L*ord,
make me an
instrument
of
your peace

Mark

Don Bolte, 59
Father
Bentonville, Arkansas

THERE ARE LOTS OF LITTLE THINGS I remember and miss about Mark. At first, every Sunday night I'd be expecting him to call because I don't think he ever missed calling on Sundays, no matter where he was. And we'd go over the sports that week together. If I had missed a game, why he'd go over it with me play by play! The year he lived in Vermont he couldn't get the Razorbacks on TV or radio, so I'd save the clippings for him and send him everything that I could find that was about the Razorbacks. The people from his work in Austin told me that if they ever had an argument about a team, all they had to do was go ask Mark! He was a walking sports encyclopedia.

He was so funny. He never wanted to change his address. His bills and stuff like that he had sent to wherever he lived, but his magazines he'd always have sent here. I'd go to the post office three or four times a month and send him his mail, mostly magazines—his *Sports Illustrated,* a football magazine, a hockey magazine, basketball guides. He wanted a copy of any guides that the University of Arkansas put out regarding sports, so I'd stop at the school and get him anything that was available. When he got to Oklahoma that's when I told him it was time to change his address. But he never got around to doing it.

I remember once when Mark was going to school in Russellville. He was getting ready to return home for Thanksgiving and the starter had gone out on the pickup he had. I tried to get him to take it to the local Chevrolet place to have it fixed. He just wouldn't do it. He said, "I want you to fix it, Dad." And so I drove to Russellville and put a starter on the truck. He was funny like that. It wasn't the money, he just trusted me to do it. I guess nobody can do it like Dad.

A characteristic of Mark's that I think is real special is the way he treated older people. Young people, I think, don't normally go out of their way to go see their grandmother a thousand miles away. On his last Easter Sunday, Mark took time and went out of his way to go to Tahlequah, Oklahoma—fifty miles from the highway—to see his Aunt Retha and to give her a flower. She still had that flower when she passed away. He always made a point of stopping to see her when he headed near that direction. Even as a child, Mark loved to go and listen to his uncle's stories. I guess he recognized that they were good, country people.

Grandma had lots of friends and he was always polite to them, even when he was smaller. When he went to work in Vermont he went out of his way to go see his grandma. And when he came back from Vermont to Texas he went up through Canada to stop in Wisconsin to see her. The summer of '94 we all met at Granny's house. Mark got there the day before we left, but he stayed on his own three more days. Mom was just remembering the other day that, although we didn't realize it at the time, after we left, Mark went over and spent the whole day just him with her. That was a great time for her to get to know him, and it meant a lot to her.

I treasure the fact that Mark and his brother Matt had grown so close. I always worried about them being so far apart in age. And when Mark left home to work and he was so far away, I worried they would get like they weren't even brothers. But it ended up the only place Matt didn't go see him was in Oregon. Matt flew up to Vermont to go skiing with him the winter he was there. He went skiing with him in Denver. He went to play golf with him in Austin. And he had already gone to Oklahoma City to see him. They got to where they were real close.

When Mark was twelve he rode sixty-five miles on his ten-speed bike for a Bike-a-thon, a fund raiser. He was biking with guys in their twenties. Wal-Mart gave away some prizes to the top winners and Mark came in third place. They had several prizes that Mark could choose from, but Mark picked out a tiny 12" bike that they had there. They all laughed at him and said, "Why do you want this little bike?" And he just said, "It's for my little brother who doesn't have a bike." That's how good he was to Matt.

One good thing is that we had gotten to see him just three days before he died. Our belief in God has given us something to hope for, knowing that there is a better place where Mark is now.

Valerie

The community of Saint Patrick Church presented Rosemary and Harry Koelsch with a collection of personal messages in memory of Valerie. The following two letters to Val were composed by her close friends, Linda and Gary Gappa.

Linda and Gary Gappa
Friends
Saint Patrick Catholic Church
Oklahoma City, Oklahoma

DEAR VAL,

We will all miss you very much! You were my rock, like a second daughter! It is very hard for me to look back behind me in Mass and not see your lovely face looking back at me. I was not ready to give you up. I guess I never will be.

When I found out that you were missing I stayed in front of the television all the time until that fateful night they found you. I know you came to me to say good-bye. When I would think of you under all that rubble I would see your little head with its beautiful bouncy hair and hear you tell me, "It's OK, Mom, I'm all right, and I'm where I need to be, doing the job I was meant to do." Val, I know you are taking care of the children and the others that are with you. It's just so hard for the ones left behind.

We had so many wonderful times together: going to see the Pope in Denver, all the cook-outs, and all the talks. I will miss the talks so very much. I know you are watching over my little family. They all love you very much. Cliff will miss the long talks about sports. Gary Lynn misses the funny little way you laughed and your beautiful smile. Lisa misses her very best friend and roommate from the World Youth Days in Denver. Gary (Pop), Patty, and I will miss all this and much more.

I know you are with God and you will not suffer heartaches or disappointments any more. You will always have a special place in my heart. I will never forget you or what you meant to me.

Your loving friend (Mom),

Linda

DEAR VALERIE,

How do I begin? Your sudden, unexpected death was such a shock to everyone. It's still hard for me to believe. There were so many things I should have told you before you were taken away from us. This letter will help me express some of those things left unsaid.

It was such a delight for me to see you at church each Sunday with your grandmother. You always had that wonderful, big smile on your face. One would have to be blind to miss it. If I happened to be ushering, you would always give me a big hug. But then, you always were one to give me a hug no matter where we were. You would always sit two or three rows behind me during Mass, and when it came time to exchange our sign of peace, we would always make eye contact and acknowledge each other with a smile or a hand shake. That always made me feel so good. Val, I am going to miss that so very much.

I need to tell you also that you were, and still are, one of my spiritual inspirations. To see you kneeling at prayer with a look of solitude and peace and detachment from your surroundings always brought to me a sense of oneness with God our Father. Dear Val, I promise to keep that image in my mind as long as I live. Isn't it amazing how we can affect people's lives and not even know it? You brought great change to my life, and I never told you.

Love, in Christ,
Gary

Julie

Lena Welch, 53
Mother
Oklahoma City, Oklahoma

I HAVE MANY PRECIOUS MEMORIES of my daughter, Julie. She was very quiet and shy as a child, but her face had a natural glow that made you like her instantly. When she was in kindergarten, the other children would tease her about her name. Since our last name is Welch, the kids gave her the nickname "Grape Juice." It upset her so much that she would come home in tears. I would tell her that one day we would laugh about such a silly name and when she was older, we did laugh about it.

Julie had a dog when she was young that she dearly loved. His name was Duffy. One day someone left the door open and Duffy got out and was killed. Heartbroken, Julie cried all night long. Unfortunately, the next day at school was picture day and her eyes were still puffy from crying. When we got the pictures back, you could see her puffy little eyes. I still have that picture.

We loved to take trips together. Julie had a tremendous thirst for knowledge and understanding. She was a foreign exchange student in Spain in high school. She then returned to Spain during her college years to once again study and understand their culture. I traveled to Spain to visit her while she was there the second time. I would walk to class with her and wait for her in the cafeteria, then we would walk back to her room and she would tell me all sorts of interesting things that she had learned. This was such a wonderful time for us and I will always treasure those memories.

In high school, when Julie was having a real hard time with things, I asked Mary every single day to show Julie the way back to the Church. I just put her in Mary's hands, and my prayers were answered. Many years later, when Julie was a senior in college, it was she who had a spiritual influence on me. When she came home during the Christmas holidays I can remember taking her to Epiphany Church because she wanted to pay a visit to the Blessed Sacrament. But the church was locked. So Julie just knelt outside, in the cold, and said her prayers.

I remember once being in the car with Julie. My mom and my brother were in town and Julie wanted us to go shopping for my mother. It was August and it was hot and I was grumpy. In the middle of it all, Julie pipes in, "anyone want to say the rosary?" My brother and my mom immediately agreed. We were saying it together but I was driving and still grumpy. Then all of a sudden, something happened and I almost ran into a car! We all broke into laughter after mother said, "maybe it's a good thing that we are saying the rosary."

Julie and I would walk together often. Frequently, she would like to say the rosary as we walked. These walks gave us time to share our lives and strengthen our bond to God. Julie was very devoted to her Catholic faith. She went to daily Mass and enjoyed saying the rosary. Christ was the center of her life and she took her spiritual development seriously. I pray to God to love her and I pray to Julie to help me through this painful time and to help make my faith stronger.

Julie and I shared a very special song. It is "You are My Sunshine." The first verse is as follows:

> *You are my sunshine, my only sunshine*
> *You make me happy, when skies are gray*
> *You'll never know dear how much I love you*
> *Please don't take my sunshine away*

Julie and I often sang this song together. It would comfort us and remind us that we always had each other. But on April 19, 1995, my sunshine was taken away. Even though she is gone, she is still with me. I sing our song and it still brings me comfort and reminds me that we will always have each other. Whenever I see a ray of sunshine, I believe it is Julie shining down on us all. I don't like to burden myself with material things. I have my faith and I have Julie in my heart and this is where I get my strength.

I look back on those last days, especially the week before it happened. It's remarkable how Julie got to say good-bye to a lot of people. Everything went so perfectly. It was Holy Week and Easter, and Julie, Eric, and I went to Muskogee together. On the way there we said the rosary together. It was the first time that Eric had visited Julie's grandma and her aunt and uncle in Muskogee. I remember on Saturday we went down to this park full of azaleas, then we went to Easter vigil at Saint Joseph's with the whole family. My mother still lives in the same house that I lived in when I was a child, next door to my sister's house. Julie went to stay the night with her grandmother while Eric and I stayed at my sister's, so my mother got to have a good visit with Julie. Mom told me they prayed together and talked about everything. On Easter Sunday Eric and Julie went back to church and took my nephews, Stephen and Andrew, with them. Julie was really at peace at this time in her life because of her closeness to God.

Julie took off on Monday to celebrate Eric's birthday. On the way to meet Eric she went by her Dad's Texaco station. She stopped an extra long time that day. Julie couldn't have had a better father. They were very close. That was the last time that he saw her. On Tuesday Julie and I met at Little Flower for Mass after work, then we went home and had a nice dinner together. Our time that week was so beautiful. It's as if one by one, she was able to say good-bye to everybody she loved.

On the morning of April 19, I remember that Julie was really excited because it was her first real Spanish-speaking claimant at Social Security. She was a bit nervous about it, but she was mostly excited. She told me she was going to Mass at Saint Charles on the way to work. As Julie prepared to leave, I was on the phone with my seventy-two-year-old mother, who had had her leg amputated the year before the bombing. She is diabetic and was having trouble with circulation in her other leg. Julie was on the way out the door while I was on the phone and she said, "I love you, Mom. Tell Grandma I love her." That's how I remember Julie. Exactly that way. She looked so pretty that morning.

Julie's body was found the Saturday after the bombing. She had a broken neck, lacerations in the face, two broken ankles . . . but we could view the body for the funeral. The other two people she was with, the claimants, were not in as good a shape and their bodies couldn't be viewed.

One night I was having a lot of trouble falling asleep. I started trying to sleep about 10 P.M. I tossed and turned and was still awake three hours later. One of my cats was playing with a newspaper that I like to read called *A Call to Peace*. It's a monthly paper about Mary and her messages around the world. At 1:50 A.M. I turned on the light and looked down on the floor where the cat was so that I could get the paper away from him and I found that the cat had Julie's rosary. I hadn't seen the rosary in a long time and I have no idea where the cat found it—maybe on the floor somewhere? I don't know. I started to cry and said "thank you" to Jesus and also to Julie. After I said about two and a half decades of the rosary I fell asleep.

Julie came from a very large Catholic family, composed of brothers, grandparents, uncles, aunts, and cousins. We all miss her very much. Julie was truly an exceptional person. She was a good daughter, a devout Catholic, and a loving woman. Her faith in God was her salvation and she helped bring her whole family closer to Him. We know that she is with God now helping Him do His work. God must need her special talents more than we do. As a parent you feel your purpose is to love and protect your children from the evil in the world. Now God will love and protect her.

Chapter 3

Where there is hatred, let me sow *love*

Mark

*Letter written by Joyce and sent from Don and Joyce Bolte on
September 3, 1996, to the families of each of the TWA plane
disaster victims:*

DEAR FAMILY,

No words can express the sorrow that you are experiencing
now and I can only say how very sorry we are and to let you
know that our prayers are with you and our hearts go out to
you every day.

We lost our eldest son Mark in the bombing in
Oklahoma City in April of 1995. He was twenty-eight years
old and had just moved there so he could be closer to home
and also have the job that he'd been seeking for five years.
He had only been in Oklahoma City since January of 1995.
We still miss him terribly and every day that goes by I still
grieve for him. But I am thankful for his life and all the wonderful memories that we have. He was a wonderful son and
a fine young man.

The terrible tragedy that took your loved one was also
a tragedy beyond comprehension. There is no deeper hurt
than to lose a loved one in such an unexpected way. It is like
one moment they are there and the next moment they are
gone. To those of you who lost more than one family
member, I can only imagine the hurt and to those of you

who are still searching, I can't even begin to know your hurt. It was two weeks before they found Mark and they were the longest and most difficult two weeks of our lives. We can only tell you that our hurt allows us to feel your pain now and to tell you that we understand.

I hope that you can lean on God and let your faith help to comfort you at this time and please do not give up on God. I know that I ask WHY? every day even though I am not supposed to. That is human nature and also a part of your grief.

I am sending you some poems that I received when Mark was killed and they have helped me a lot and maybe they will bring some comfort to you, too. Remember that there are many people praying for you and asking God to help you through this most devastating time in your life.

Love and sympathy,
Don and Joyce Bolte
Bentonville, Arkansas

Valerie

T. J. Garis, 34
Friend
Dallas, Texas

THERE ARE VERY FEW GENUINE PEOPLE in the world, and Valerie was one of them. Always sincere, Val was one of the sweetest people I have ever met. As a role model, Valerie was a very true, loving, and caring person. She didn't have a mean bone in her body.

I knew Valerie through playing softball. We also grew up and went to school together. Valerie and I were always being "silly." We would be the two sitting in the back of a team meeting laughing and trying to keep from making too much noise. Valerie and I had nicknames for each other: she was "Brother Bob" and I was "Brother Bill." Who knows where we got that from! I remember when we were young how we used to meet at Valerie's house on the weekend and play football—we both loved it.

When Valerie's name comes to mind I see her with a big smile on her face. I can't picture Valerie without a smile on her face. And when I think of the two of us, I see us side by side, giggling, smiling, and having fun.

I see Valerie in my dreams. To some this might sound strange, but I believe it is her way to see me. Every time I see Valerie, she comes to tell me "hello" with her big smile. She lets me know that she is fine and that things are great. I truly believe that she comes into my dreams to see me. And each time I see her it's a very happy meeting, just like old friends who live a little far away and are reunited.

The first time Valerie appeared in my dreams it was to let me know she was okay, and that we shouldn't be sad or become hateful. This helped me a lot, knowing that she was in good hands, that she was in God's hands. Each time she comes to see me, it is short but I wake up with a smile on my face.

Julie

Ruby Mae Compassi, 73
Grandmother
Muskogee, Oklahoma

JULIE MARIE WAS MY OLDEST GRANDDAUGHTER. A very
kind, generous, sincere, and loving person, she spoke Spanish
fluently and worked to help the Spanish speaking people
with their Social Security problems in Oklahoma City. I'm
proud that she worked hard at what she did.

Julie wondered about her ancestors, who they were and
what their nationality was. My folks drifted here from New
York. They were German and French. My husband, who
came over here from the old country, was in the seminary
over in Italy. He was about four years away from becoming a
priest when he came to the United States. He couldn't speak
English, and that made it real hard for him. Then he met and
married me. I guess it's just kind of natural for Julie to have
such devotion to Jesus and His Church, like her Grandpa,
who always stayed close to the Church up to his death twenty years ago. And, he always encouraged the children to stay
close to their Church. And none of them have really fallen
away. And if they did, they came back. You know, if you
keep praying—they come back.

Julie came to visit me for Easter of 1995, three days
before she died. That weekend, she brought her boyfriend
Eric Hilz down to my home in Muskogee for the first time.
We went to church and had a nice dinner together. Julie
asked me, "Grandma, how do you like my boyfriend?" I last
saw Julie alive on that Easter Sunday. I did get to talk with

her again, on the day she died. On her way to work on April 19 Julie told me on the telephone, "Grandma, I love you!"

Julie went to Mass very often and received the sacraments of reconciliation and Holy Communion often. She prayed the rosary with me and had a special devotion to the Blessed Virgin Mary and to Jesus. If Julie were here, she'd want to tell people that she forgives those responsible for the bombing because that's what Christ had to do, forgive people. She would not like anyone to have hate in their hearts, and she'd probably ask us to pray for the people who killed her and all those other innocent people.

Julie would come down every holiday. Seems like it's not really the same now that she's gone—we're at a loss without her. She just really made our holidays, Julie did. We thought she was real grand, our wonderful little 'ole girl.

While we waited for Julie to be found we were looking for a miracle because she was a very special miracle baby. She was born prematurely and it's a miracle she survived. We'd give everything under the sun to have our little ray of sunshine here with us again. We think she was just about the grandest person we've ever seen. Nothing could replace her.

Chapter 4

Where there is injury, let me sow *pardon*

Mark

Bruce A. Lind, 55
Co-worker
Federal Highway Administration
Oklahoma City, Oklahoma

I MET MARK FOR THE FIRST TIME in December of 1994 when he visited our Federal Highway Administration offices on a house-hunting trip to Oklahoma City. He moved to Oklahoma City in January of 1995 and rented an apartment in the northwest part of the city. Mark joined a car pool consisting of Mike Herron, Rick Tomlin (both FHWA employees), and myself. Eleven of our employees, including Rick and Mark, were killed in the bombing.

Riding to and from work every day, we all got to know each other pretty well. One of our more frequent topics of conversation revolved around Scouts, as Mark was an Eagle Scout and I was Scout Master of Boy Scout Troop 177. Eagle is the Boy Scouts' highest rank—only two or three percent of the boys who join Scouts ever reach it. That says a lot about the determination and character of those who do. Eagle rank is for life, and with it comes the implied obligation that those who reach this rank will be active supporters of the Scouts in adulthood.

Mark exemplified the meaning of Eagle Scout. He soon volunteered to be an adult leader for Troop 177 and was an instant hit with the boys. When Mark learned that the troop was planning a canoe trip at the Boy Scouts' Canoe Base in northern Minnesota, he provided us with information and practical advice to make the trip easier and more enjoyable. Mark had made the same trip as a youth. Just prior to the bombing, Mark had brought his Scouting mementos to Oklahoma City from his family's home in Arkansas to show the boys, but he died before he had the chance to show them. Because of his attitude and his disposition, Mark had a profound impact on the boys and adult leaders of Troop 177. He was a soft-spoken gentleman who lived the Scout Oath and Law and led by example. He understood the importance of that. Mark exemplified the adult Eagle Scout and took its responsibilities seriously. Mark was a young man and the boys could relate to him, although he was large in stature. He treated everyone, but particularly the boys, with great respect. Everything about him said, "Here is an Eagle Scout." When the troop replaced its old troop flag, the new one was dedicated to his memory.

Mark was very well liked at the office and by his counterparts at the Oklahoma Department of Transportation (ODOT). He had a confident good-naturedness that allowed him to make friends easily and to win their respect as a competent engineer. Mark served as the environmental coordinator for our office. In this capacity he was often placed in situations with persons who had strong but very different points of view. The situation with the ODOT that Mark encountered upon arriving in Oklahoma was very strained. But he quickly turned it into a positive and cooperative working relationship. He was a good listener who could identify areas of common interest and compromise and use those to build consensus among the parties.

On the morning of April 19, Mike Herron was on vacation and Rick Tomlin had driven into work by himself. Mark and I were the only ones in the car pool that morning. The last time I can remember seeing Mark was as we were walking into the office together. I remember Mark as a happy good-natured young man who was always looking for ways to help. His dedication and sense of duty to his Church and to the Boy Scouts make him an outstanding role model for young people.

Valerie

Kristi Mohr, 31
Friend, Youth Director
Saint Mary's Catholic Church
Ponca City, Oklahoma

VALERIE'S LIFE AND DEATH have had a profound impact on my life. After my separation (and subsequent divorce) from my ex-husband, God led me to places and people within His Church. One person was Valerie and one place was Saint Charles Borromeo Catholic Church, where I began playing volleyball with the young adults. Soon, I was part of the community.

My parents attended Mount Saint Mary Catholic High School with Valerie's parents and, over the years, my family and Valerie's family would get together occasionally. But it was in this difficult period of my life, as adults, that our friendship developed. It was Val and her friend, Kim Whaylen, who started inviting me into their young adult activities for the Archdiocese of Oklahoma City. Val's passion for sports was like her passion for the other things in life that had great importance to her: God, her Church, her family, and her friends. I was always impressed by Val's commitment to her family. She made great efforts to spend time with her family, and I was touched on several occasions when I saw her taking her grandmother to church. I remember countless occasions when she visited her brother's family in Texas, and I remember the many times that she spent with her sister, Michelle, and her family. Val loved children and wanted so much to be married. The fact that she never got that opportunity really caused a lot of grief for me after her death. It was sadness at realizing that someone had robbed Val of her dreams. She is undoubtedly one of the people who led me back to a fuller participation in the Church. And consequently, led me on a new road in my faith and life journey.

Through our shared experiences at World Youth Day in Denver, Val and I developed an even deeper friendship. At World Youth Day, she was like a little kid who marveled at everything. She was full of anticipation even before we went at the whole idea of a World Youth Day and she could hardly wait to get there. Her childlike excitement stirred up the people around her. It was contagious.

Val and I walked around together a lot at World Youth Day. I remember we ran into Father Michael Chapman and Father Scott Adams. At one point Val and I went over the hill and looked over the Masses of people. Val remarked how "this must have been what it was like when Jesus was walking the earth!" And we discussed how there must have been thousands of people captivated by Jesus' presence. And how our Pope has a similar presence in our world today. We were overwhelmed at seeing how many people really love the Church. Val was absolutely elated when the Pope's plane entered the area of the Mile High Stadium. She was amazed by the size and enthusiasm of the crowd at the Mass in Cherry Park, as was I.

That Saturday night in Cherry Hill State Park, they raised a huge banner of the Risen Lord that went up by a crane over the west. The banner was rolled up, so when it was unfolded it started at his feet and opened up slowly until it got to Jesus' head. Val was so thrilled! I'll never forget her excitement—her eyes were bright, her hands were moving, and her body was almost dancing. You could definitely see it in her face. And she said out loud, "Oh my gosh, look at that! It's so incredible!" Val was overjoyed. And the irony is that I would not even have noticed the banner if Valerie hadn't pointed it out. A few months ago, Val's mom gave me a prayer card that says "Jesus I trust you" that Valerie had hanging on her mirror at home. The image is similar to the one we saw that day, with Jesus' hands raised. She was truly overwhelmed by that particular theme. There's part of me that finds comfort in that.

Later that year Valerie also talked me into becoming a member of the core team for the Young Adult Ministry at the Archdiocese. Consequently, she and I went on several trips together, as well as retreats. One of those trips was to a Young Adult Conference in Colorado Springs in December of 1994. I hadn't intended to go, but Val and my mother talked me into it. I knew at that point that God wanted me there for a reason. What I didn't know was that that conference would have an incredible impact on our lives, especially mine.

When Valerie and I came back from Colorado Springs, we both knew that there was something important in life! Namely, God and His work. Valerie and I discussed the effects that the conference had on us several times afterwards. I think that she was really struggling with those effects in the fact that she liked her job at the credit union, and it paid well, but something in her (God) was convincing her that there was something more important, more fulfilling. I understood because I felt it too! I believe that she might have eventually changed careers to work for the Church if she had been given the opportunity.

A year after Val's death, I had an opportunity to leave my job at Presbyterian Hospital in Oklahoma City where I was making decent money as an employment recruiter and change to the position of youth director at Saint Mary's Catholic Church in Ponca City. I really wanted to make the change but had some fears: would I be able to make it on two-thirds of what I made at Presbyterian? The conversations Valerie and I had after Colorado Springs in combination with her violent death gave me the courage to move into this new chapter in my life. I knew I needed to make the sacrifice of leaving family, friends, and money in order to follow my heart and respond to the Lord. I wanted to be God's instrument in helping, teaching, and loving teens in order that they might not choose the same desperate road of hate that the perpetrator of the OKC bombing had chosen.

At Val's funeral, the grief was overwhelming and the pain intense as I watched Harry and Rosemary push her coffin out of the church, but I will also never forget how spiritually glorious that day was for me. There was joy within me because I knew Valerie was home, and because I was able to witness the magnitude of the lives touched by Val. As my friends and I drove to the funeral I explained to them that I always liked sunshine on funeral days because it was my reminder of God's presence. However, the day they buried Val was a very rainy, gray day. The church was packed full of the people that loved Val and had come to say good-bye: Archbishop Beltran, several priests, family members, church friends, school friends from Saint Gregory's and Putnam City, sport friends, and work friends. I was amazed at how many were affected by her loss. I remember thinking that her life must have glorified God because she shared His love with so many, and in return others loved her. During the funeral at Saint Patrick Church, where light is allowed in through the glass walls, beams of sun found their way into the funeral Mass. It was at that moment that I found a smile and experienced the joy within me of knowing Val was in God's care.

I realize that some of the greatest experiences I have had in the past several years have been shared with Valerie Koelsch and the Catholic Church. The last time I saw Valerie was a week before the bombing when she invited me to attend a teaching Mass at Saint Eugene Church with Father Rick Stansberry. Afterwards, we ate dinner with Father Bill Pruett and during the conversation, I remember Valerie saying that, "after Colorado Springs, I know that there is something more." I never imagined that she'd be part of that something more—Heaven—one week later. Her statement that day gave me the courage a year later to move to Ponca City in order to minister to youth in the Church that I love.

And the consequences of the bombing and the loss of Val have thrust me into a whole new life with a new perspective on the value and preciousness of life, the love of God, and a new list of priorities. The loss of her creates an emptiness within me, yet my Catholic faith allows me the opportunity to share with her in the communion of saints. I have felt her presence many times over the past two years. I still miss her and grieve her death, but I find consolation and hope as I look forward to our reunion in Heaven!

Julie

Erin Wright, 25
Friend, freelance journalist
Iowa City, Iowa

JULIE AND I MET THROUGH A FRIEND of a friend when I was seventeen and in my freshman year at Marquette. But I did not really get to know Julie until she came back from spending a year in Spain. By coincidence, she was moving into an apartment above mine on Fourteenth Street. We were both very alone. We each had our own apartment for the first time, we didn't really know anybody else in our building, and we became very good friends. There was a security there in our friendship. We were living in a nasty neighborhood and, if I didn't come home some night, I needed somebody to notice. Sometimes when she came home she'd stop at my door before she went all the way upstairs to her apartment and we'd sit down, have a cigarette, and just talk about the day. Back then, Julie was a smoker and so was I. It became so comfortable that when my friends and family needed to reach me they could call her, and Bud and her family knew they were welcome to call for her at my place.

Julie left Marquette and went back to Oklahoma City for a while. She was facing a lot of issues and she needed to be at home. After she left, we didn't really talk to each other very much until she moved back—almost a year later—and the two of us moved in together. But Julie and I did not get along. We were both dealing with a lot of questions in our lives and we drove each other nuts. We were roommates for about six months until I left Marquette and moved back home to Iowa. I left with some unresolved tension between us and I never had an opportunity to resolve that with her, much to my regret. That's a lot of weight to carry.

While Julie and I were roommates, I was going to a Bible study at the Joan of Arc Chapel on campus and I was struggling with my Catholic faith. The priest who led the Bible study was from this tiny church up in North Milwaukee. Although Julie never really got involved with the Bible study itself, she did come with me to church. But even in that, we were at different places in our faith. I don't want to judge Julie's faith—but I would say that hers was much stronger than mine, or at least, she was much more willing to practice all of the Catholic traditions as well as have a strong faith. And I was struggling with Catholicism as my faith.

Julie changed a lot during college. I remember her as being very left, perhaps radical liberal as a freshman. She very seldom went to church; she very seldom talked about God. She did, but as much or as little as the rest of us. The group we hung out with included all kinds of alternative or funky lifestyles—musicians, a dancer, an artist, a loafer—but our common thread was acceptance. We were a very intelligent bunch of kids, all interested in classic debate and learning from each other. We tried very hard to be socially responsible. It was just a neat bunch of folks.

To this group of people Julie was a very different person when she came back from her year away from Marquette. She had changed dramatically. She was not interested in a lot of the things that she had been interested in before. Julie's faith was growing rapidly, and she began to judge other people's actions in the group and that was tough. Before then, we didn't always agree, we didn't always like every aspect of each other, but we had respect for each other and our own individual lifestyles. When she returned to Milwaukee, Julie was a lot more judgmental about faith and less tolerant of the actions of those of us who weren't as committed as she was. This was not in an absolute sense—Julie was very kindhearted and she was very giving. From the moment I met her to the last time I saw her, that did not change. But Julie was disappointed and she came down like a hammer on some of the people in our group. One of our members led a bisexual life and Julie very clearly let everybody know that that was not acceptable.

There were so many of us who loved Julie and who tried so hard to understand her new life. We gave her 100 percent support, but we didn't always understand what her goals were. It was like learning a new person. She was growing up and we didn't know how to react.

I really supported Julie's faith. I encouraged her to talk to me about her beliefs and we had lots of conversations about God because I was very interested. And a lot of beliefs we did share. Julie was growing in her faith a lot faster than I was. And I was learning from her in that way. I think Julie and I worked on each other. Ironically, before Julie left for her year away in Oklahoma City, I had witnessed to Julie with a pamphlet about making God the center of our lives. I went over it with Julie the best way I understood it. I said, "We're not going to get to heaven by doing good deeds, by trying not to swear, or by leading a good lifestyle, but through our faith in Jesus. Once we accept that, then all the other things fall into place." It was rather ironic that I would be the one to share with Julie and then, at the end, Julie was the one who had the stronger faith. I don't know if she would credit me with the onset of that. I don't know how much of an effect that had on her. At the time, I thought it was a pretty strong effect.

Losing Julie has made me think a lot about the people who are close to me. Julie and I drove each other nuts, but we had a lot of good times. And I miss her. If I could speak with her now, I'd say, "You drove me nuts, but I love you anyway." I probably would say that I'm sorry because I didn't make her transition back to Marquette easy. I tried, but I didn't know how. It's hard to care for somebody else when you can't care for yourself.

I got a call on April 19 that Julie had been in the Murrah Building, but I didn't find out until Sunday that she had been killed. It didn't hit me right away that she'd been killed, but when it did, I started shaking. Many of us traveled from all over to be with Bud and Lena—from Boston, Pittsburgh, Houston, Cincinnati, Denver, and Iowa City. The funeral gave us a chance to remember Julie and offer support to one another. It was like that line from *Fiddler on the Roof*, "I'll walk, I'll crawl, I'll get there!"

It is ironic that the Julie that we all knew and loved was a Julie we saw as insecure. It was just very ironic that Julie had to die to see how much all of us genuinely cared. I don't think she ever quite believed it. When we were at the funeral we couldn't help but say, "This is it, here you go—do you see this? This church full of people from all over the country." It was like we came down in buses and droves. And people I never thought would be there, were there. We came because this was somebody who touched our lives in such a special way. This was somebody we would never forget. I really hope she realized before she died how influential she really was.

I tried to honor Julie's memory by singing the "Ave Maria" a capella at the rosary. I was so scared. I kept praying, "Ok, God. Keep me intact. Keep my wits about me. Allow me this chance to do this and then I'll cry." I got up there and introduced myself and said what I was going to do— because Julie had often sought Mary's guidance and often said the rosary. And it seemed like every note was perfect. With God's help, I sang better than I had ever sung before. When I stepped down, that's when I lost it. I cried like a baby. God let me get through that and then I could mourn.

During the funeral Mass, the priest unexpectedly asked all the Marquette people to bring down the gifts. You have to understand the humor in this. One of the most rewarding things about our gaggle of friends is its diversity. Our group of people is made up of people who are all very different. Some of us are strictly religious (usually Catholic), some of us were recovering, some practiced once in a while, some were atheists, and some, like me, were moderate yet practicing Catholics. You can imagine the wave of looks we gave each other in the pew as the priest made his request.

I'm not sure who it was who finally gave me the chalice, but I led this motley crew down the aisle. Angelically, we all genuflected at the same time. Only God could see the tarnish on our halos. It was a funny thing that we were all in church. Later, at the hotel, we remembered how Julie vowed to get us all in church—one way or the other, we knew she was going to do it.

We never imagined it would be at her funeral.

Chapter 5

Where there is doubt, let me sow *faith*

Mark

Guy Wilkerson, 69
Leader (41 years)
Boy Scout Troop 52
Bentonville, Arkansas

I MET MARK BOLTE when he was eleven years old and his father dropped him off to join the Boy Scouts. Mark was always an eager beaver to learn. He also wanted to teach what he had learned to other boys in his patrol or troop.

Mark served in many capacities while a member of Troop 52, becoming an Eagle Scout, the highest rank in the Boy Scouts. He was presented his Eagle at the Rogers, Arkansas, Catholic Church where he was also a member.

I recall that as a patrol leader Mark was in a contest at a camp-out to see that his patrol cooked a chicken dinner, including all the trimmings. His patrol offered many challenges to Mark. As he was trying to build a fire, his people would blow it out. They had trouble getting the water and his gravy was not a work of art. But Mark never quit.

I also remember that Mark and several of his friends all started college at the same time. Mark was the only one to complete his major in the same field that he started. I have to say this: Mark always completed any project or assignment that was given to him. And did so in an extraordinary way.

Mark had determination. He would make happen whatever he set his mind to. That to me was his best quality.

Mark was dependable, he was just about the same all the time. If you knew him you'd know what he would do or wouldn't do. Mark was also an example as an altar boy at church. He was a great influence on others. And he was everything the Church could probably have wanted.

Any kind remark you can say about somebody I want to say about Mark. Mark was an outstanding person, a really good person. He was a benefit to his generation.

Valerie

Kim Whaylen, 34
Friend
Bethany, Oklahoma

Val and I knew each other since junior high school when we played on opposing softball teams. We went to the same high school but didn't really get to know each other until we attended Saint Gregory's College in Shawnee, Oklahoma, together. It was there that we became great friends.

Val and I shared so many good times together that there are lots of things that remind me of her daily. Of course, anything that speaks of OSU (Oklahoma State University) says "Val" all over it! She was such a big fan of OSU sports. In fact, I remember one party that we went to together—we were sitting in the backyard talking and having a good time and it was time for some kind of OSU ball

game to come on the TV. Val hooked up a TV on the deck
and was in her own zone as she watched the game while the
rest of us kept talking! We went to numerous football games
together in Stillwater, always with a side trip to Eskimo Joe's!
We also attended several of Eskimo Joe's anniversary parties
that took place every year in July. When they added on to
Joe's, they placed a time capsule in the ground. The plaque
on the time capsule stated that it was to be opened on Joe's
fiftieth anniversary. Val and I figured out that we would be
in our 60's at that time, and we agreed that we would be
there together for the opening of the capsule no matter
where we were in our lives.

While we attended Saint Gregory's College, Val and I
made several friends who lived in Chicago. Some of my
fondest memories of Val include the trips we took to
Chicago together to attend the weddings of these friends. We
were always labeled "the girls from Oklahoma" and we were
welcomed with open arms. We loved attending these big
Catholic weddings and were planning ours patterned on
these Chicago weddings. As you know, Val never married
and I haven't yet, but there will be an empty place in my
wedding someday, because she won't be there.

If you ask anyone who knew Val, her smile and laughter would be something they would talk about immediately.
She laughed a lot! And when she did, her whole body would
shake as she laughed! And her smile—Val's smile would light
up the room.

Val's faith was very important to her, as was evident by
her involvement at her church, Saint Patrick's, and with the
Young Adult Group. She was a founding member of that
group and she spent lots of time working with it. I know that

being involved in the Church was very important to Val. Once, Val and I attended the funeral of a friend that happened to be a priest's brother. After the funeral, we talked about the number of priests who were there—and Val mentioned how cool it would be to have several priests celebrate hers someday. I know Val had to be pleased with the number of priests she had at hers!

I'm sure you have heard by now how important Val's family was to her. Spending time with her family meant a great deal to her. She was so excited about being an aunt, and she loved taking her nieces to different places. Val talked about them constantly and had pictures of them all over her refrigerator.

One of the best times Val and I had together was on our trip to the World Youth Day in Denver. We were two of the young adults that took the trip and we just had a fabulous time. It meant so much to both of us to see the Pope so close and to listen to people from other parts of the world speak. Val and I talked about that trip for a long time. It boosted our spirituality and it made us fall in love with the Catholic Church all over again.

Julie

M. Sharon Hefferan, 40
Petawa Residence, Director
Milwaukee, Wisconsin

I REMEMBER JULIE AS A SMILING, friendly, spunky girl who wore a helmet while riding her bike!—she loved to ride her bike. I also remember her as a caring person who was able to relate to and deal with people of all ages and who had a special gift for talking to and appreciating older people. This could explain why she loved her grandparents so much. At Petawa we have an eighty-three-year-old woman on our staff named Rose. Julie loved to talk with Rose, and even asked Rose to teach her piano a few months before graduation. Julie would plug away at her simple scales day after day and by the time she left in August she even had down a few easy tunes!

Despite the fact that Julie's parents were separated, Julie managed to maintain a loving relationship with both her mom and her dad. I think this is important to note because many young people who come from family situations like Julie's don't always know how to deal with this challenge. Nevertheless, for as long as I knew her, Julie always made the effort to call and write both sides of her family. This again is a testimony to her ability to be concerned for others rather than thinking of herself and her own personal or emotional needs. Only a generous soul can achieve this level of self-sacrifice and charity.

One incident that I think exemplifies how Julie put the needs of others above her own interests was the decision she made concerning life after college. When it came time to graduate, Julie—like most college grads—had to make the big decisions about what to do, where to work, and where to live. She had been a dedicated Spanish major and had worked locally in Milwaukee for a few years. She had as good an opportunity as other Marquette grads to find a job in Milwaukee. She told me, however, that as much as she would like to stay local and keep in touch with the programs and people at Petawa, she felt deep down that her family (Mom, Dad, and grandmothers) needed her back in Oklahoma City. It was a tough decision for her, but she made it prayerfully and had a lot of peace about it. She looked forward to moving back home, but she also had career options, friends and connections in Milwaukee that were hard for her to say good-bye to. We both trusted that God would help her find a way in OKC to use her college education, find a job, and to keep up her practice of the faith while at the same time being a support to her family. As she had decided, she relocated back home in August of 1994 after spending the summer with us at Petawa and working for a short time longer in Milwaukee. Often in college you build up hopes and dreams of "the big career" and of putting your degree to use. Julie had not lost that. She had tremendous professional zeal and a great desire to use her Spanish major for the benefit of many, which she did at the Social Security Administration. But she decided that her family's needs came before her friends and before other professional opportunities.

The spring of 1994, Julie attended an Opus Dei retreat for college girls at Shellbourne Conference Center in Valparaiso, Indiana. Julia Wolff invited her, and I accompanied her as part of the staff. At the end of the retreat, those of us organizing it gave the participants who were interested the opportunity to have the scapular of Our Lady of Mount Carmel imposed. Julie told me that she didn't think that she had ever had it imposed and that she would like to be included in the simple ceremony. During the ceremony the priest gave an explanation of the benefits of having a devotion to Our Lady of Mount Carmel and the Sabbatine privilege, which is Mary's promise to take to heaven the first

Saturday after their death any of the faithful who wear the scapular with devotion. I remember from that day on Julie wore her scapular faithfully. A little more than one year later, Julie died in the bombing. Her mother Lena told me that they had identified Julie's body at the morgue on Saturday morning about noon and that, even though she died of a broken neck, she still had her scapular lying on her chest! From that day on I realized the importance of introducing young people to this devotion, and I gave thanks that Julie had the opportunity to discover this devotion that God would use only a little over a year later to snatch her up to heaven.

I realize that her faith is a delicate subject. Many of Julie's friends whom I met at her funeral—and who knew her before I did—said that the "Catholic girl with conviction" that they were hearing about at the funeral was a "different Julie, not the one they knew." Of course, I knew the Julie they were talking about, the typical college kid who connected with a bad crowd and was pulled along by the vices that tempt all of us at that age. Nevertheless, I also knew the new Julie that began blossoming shortly before she moved into Petawa, who grew tremendously by developing a solid prayer and sacramental life while she was at Petawa, the Julie who connected with the rosary group at her parish in OKC, which had helped her so much.

Julie is a role model of someone who knew how to count on the sacraments of penance and the Eucharist and who could seek advice from others practicing their faith, to guide her in her spiritual life. I firmly believe that it was Julie's trust in sacramental grace and her effort to receive the sacraments of penance and the Eucharist frequently that helped her obtain the strength to fix what needed changing in her life. She sought out spiritual direction from Opus Dei, which helped her reinforce these desires for change and growth by concretizing small practical goals to work on in her spiritual life. Julie progressed slowly but surely on the new life of faith that was taking place within her. I know that Julie would agree with me on this point because she herself observed how these two sacraments helped her turn her life around and helped her develop a faith that was expressed in prayer and deeds.

Julie's awakening to return to a regular practice of the faith, I believe, was due to the efforts of Justin and Julia Wolff and the prayers of her mom, dad, and grandparents. Justin and Julia would invite her to daily Mass with them and would then explain the faith and answer her questions for hours on end. The three of them had a wonderful friendship. Then Julia brought Julie to Petawa. Julie started coming to our programs for college girls. I believe that Julia helped prepare Julie for the sacrament of penance, which Julie had not taken advantage of for several years. Once Julie moved into Petawa, she made the effort to tap in on the grace of the sacrament of penance by going to confession almost weekly. More than once Julie commented to me that having the opportunity to receive this sacrament with regularity, and to use it as a tool for beginning again in her spiritual life, was a tremendous consolation to her.

The last time I saw Julie was the day she left Petawa in August of 1994. We kept in touch by letter from time to time. Julie's most endearing quality in my mind was her genuine concern for others, exhibited by her generous spirit of service. This character strength was shown in so many ways in life at Petawa, from offering to help with the dishes on week-ends, to shuttling other Marquette students from Petawa to Marquette in her shiny red Grand Am—which I might add she took very good care of. Her interest in the daily affairs (sorrows and joys) of others was shown by her inquisitive and spontaneous questions, like "How was your day?" But when Julie asked, she *meant* it, and she waited for the person to respond with a story or even just a comment.

Chapter 6

Where there is despair, let me sow *hope*

Mark

"Boy next door among last bombing victims found"

*Article in the **Arkansas Catholic** newspaper of the Diocese of Little Rock May 13, 1995 by Betsy McNeil*

THE CHAPEL AT CALLISON-LOUGH Funeral Home in Rogers was overflowing at a prayer service Monday, May 8, for former Bentonville resident Mark Bolte.

For more than 90 minutes, friends and family lined up to say good-bye to the twenty-eight-year-old native son.

Father Mike Sinkler, assistant pastor at Saint Vincent de Paul Church in Rogers and Saint Stephen Mission in Bentonville, officiated, and was assisted by Deacon Clarence Leis.

Bolte was the last Federal Highway Administration employee pulled from the rubble caused by the April 19 bombing of the Alfred P. Murrah Federal Building in Oklahoma City. His body was recovered on Thursday, May 3, a few hours before the official search was called off.

A portrait of Mark, a civil engineer and environmental specialist, was placed beside his blue casket, along with the awards and certificates he had earned as a Knights of the Altar Server and Eagle Scout. A bulletin board nearby displayed a letter of condolence from a former college professor, photographs, and other mementos. Bolte and his family—parents Don and Joyce and brother Matt—are members at Saint Vincent de Paul Church in Rogers.

"If there ever was a perfect son, Mark Bolte was it," said family friend Gloria Moore. "Everybody has faults, but I couldn't name you one that Mark had. He was liked by everyone."

Moore's husband, Donnie, agreed.

"Mark was the boy next door," he said. "That's the only way to describe him. He always helped younger kids, that was his deal. He helped everybody."

According to his mother, Mark Bolte was a "good boy." He never missed Mass, and he was one to send greeting cards to "everyone for all occasions."

During college, he would return to Rogers to attend the annual altar servers banquet, and every Christmas, he would serve at midnight Mass alongside other Knights of the Altar alumni, including his brother Matt.

Hired by the Federal Highway Administration in January 1991, Bolte trained and worked in North Carolina, Oregon, Colorado, Vermont, and Austin, Texas. He assumed his current position and moved to Oklahoma City on January 22, 1995. In the short time he lived in Oklahoma, he had signed on as an assistant scout master, and was preparing to join the young adults group at his parish, Epiphany of the Lord Church.

His father and brother ushered at Mass on Easter this year. Mark Bolte sat with his mother. That Sunday was the last time the family saw him alive.

"He called about 8 P.M. to let us know he had arrived home safely," Don Bolte said. "Mark always did that, he called so we wouldn't worry."

After hearing about the bombing, the Bolte family was summarily summoned to Oklahoma City to await word on Mark. They spent their nights in Mark's apartment.

During that time, they were ministered to by Father Lowell Stieferman, Mark's pastor, and Father David Monahan, former editor of the *Sooner Catholic*, who was associated with the Epiphany of the Lord Church.

One aspect of Mark's personal life that perhaps will be forever etched in Father Stieferman's memory was a well-worn Bible.

"The family showed me the Bible," the priest said. "He obviously had read it a lot. As I opened it, there were two bookmarks. One was in the book of Judges, the other was at the beginning of the Gospel of Mark."

The Boltes grew close to one woman—Gabriella Aleman—whose husband was among the missing.

"We worried more about Gabby than we did ourselves," Joyce Bolte said. "She was really having a hard time. She has a 3-year-old girl and a 6-month-old boy."

As a token of friendship, Aleman presented the Boltes with a gold guardian angel pin decorated with ribbons. The idea of wearing a lapel pin quickly caught on. An assembly line of victims' family members began producing the multi-colored mementos for the firemen, police officers and rescue workers at the site. Yellow represented hope, purple stood for children, blue was for Oklahoma, and white as a reminder of those who were still missing.

When the guardian angels became hard to find in Oklahoma, Joyce Bolte, an employee at the Wal-Mart general office in Bentonville, made one call to the home office. That was all it took before 400 angel pins from Wal-Mart in Chickasha were donated.

The family was officially notified of their son's death late Thursday afternoon. After waiting 15 days for the news, it came as almost a relief.

"We thought we were going to have to come home without him," Joyce Bolte said.

The Boltes remained filled with gratitude and thanksgiving for the numerous acts of kindness they experienced and witnessed. Still stunned by the tragedy and by the loss of their son, they are relying on their faith to carry them through the days ahead.

"Having a Catholic background and our belief in God gave us something to hope for," Don Bolte said. "Knowing that if we did lose Mark, there is a better place for him to go."

Valerie

Terry Koelsch, 36
Brother
Arlington, Texas

I NEVER IMAGINED HOW ONE WEEK in April could change my life forever. And how, in her last five days on earth,

Valerie would have the opportunity to see and to share with every member of her family.

Saturday, April 15, 1995, brought great joy as my second daughter, Taylor Reneé, was born. This was a significant date because three years earlier, on the exact day, my first daughter, Kayla Nicole, was born. Later, I would learn how fortunate it was that God allowed them to come into this world on the same day.

Friday, April 14, after a week of anticipating this new addition to the family, my wife, Rhonda, and I accepted the fact that our baby would probably not arrive for another week. This was fine because we were busy getting ready for Kayla's birthday party on Saturday at McDonald's. Everything was ready. My parents Harry Joe and Rosemary, my sister Valerie, and my niece Laurie, were all scheduled to make the trip from Oklahoma City to Arlington, Texas, to attend the birthday party on Saturday. Excitement and anticipation filled the house that night. It wasn't until 11:30 P.M. that Kayla finally shut her eyes and went to sleep.

At midnight, Rhonda's water broke and we knew it was time to go to the hospital. Luckily, Rhonda's mother, Jane Bryant, had arrived earlier that evening. She stayed with Kayla as we left to go deliver the baby. I was inwardly chuckling as we looked at each other and said, "They're going to have the same birthday!" And I was thankful that most of our relatives had already scheduled to be there for Kayla's birthday and that they would get to see the new baby.

The delivery was slow and, by noon, we still hadn't progressed very far. My parents, Valerie, and Laurie had arrived from Oklahoma City, so I asked them if they would run Kayla's birthday party. They met Grandma Jane and

Kayla and went to McDonald's at 3:00 P.M. At 4:32, Taylor was born. We were so very happy. My father-in-law, Bear Bryant, arrived just in time to be the first to hold Taylor. We took lots of pictures and every one held her. It was great having so much family there.

Sunday came, and my father, Valerie, Laurie, and my in-laws had to go back to Oklahoma. My mother stayed to help, and now, looking back, I wish Valerie had stayed, too. Once in Oklahoma City, Dad, Val, and Laurie went to the hospital to see my niece, Lindsey, who was recovering from an asthma attack. There they returned Laurie to her parents.

On Monday, back at work at the Credit Union, Valerie was the proud aunt, showing pictures of her new niece to everyone. At lunch, she again showed them to one of her best friends, Agnes Berkenbile.

Tuesday, Val left her office for the afternoon to attend a meeting in Tulsa. Upon arrival, she discovered they had canceled her meeting. So that the trip would not be a total loss, she dropped by to see a good friend, Stephanie, who worked in the same building. Stephanie later told us that after a short visit, Valerie gave her a long hug as she said good-bye. Val then drove to Edmond, Oklahoma, to visit her sister and brother-in-law, Michelle and Gary Brooks, and their seven-month-old son, Austin. Looking back at those days now, we're grateful that Val was able to see and spend time with all of her immediate family. She brought Austin an Easter toy, which they will long treasure. A church meeting was her plan for that evening. Then off to work Wednesday morning with plans to go to Stillwater, Oklahoma, for OSU baseball on the weekend.

Wednesday morning found us up early in Texas, playing with the two girls and watching the news. Suddenly, a special report flashed on the screen. The explosion had occurred forty minutes earlier. My mom immediately broke into tears saying, "That's Val's building!" Knowing her office was on the west side of the third floor credit union, she feared the worst. Little did we know at the time that a staff meeting would put her in the part of the building that was hardest hit. Terror filled our faces as I grabbed the phone to call my dad. The phone was dead. Earlier storms in Arlington had caused a problem in our phone line. I was running around not knowing what to do. We continued to watch the report in utter shock. Finally my wife suggested I go next door to call my father. After several tries, I finally got through. His voice made me realize that he knew the situation. Minutes before the blast, he had left his shop, a few miles from downtown, to head to a job on the south part of town. He felt the bomb and thought a tanker truck had exploded on the highway. But the closer he got to downtown Oklahoma City, he realized it was a building. With horror, he recognized it as the Federal Building where his eldest daughter was employed. He frantically drove closer. It was four minutes after the explosion and already all roads leading to the building were blocked off. My father, reluctantly, drove back to his office. A call on his company radio came from the receptionist, telling him to come back to the shop and see her immediately. She didn't think he had knowledge of the bombing.

In a cracking voice, I heard my father tell me to sit tight, that there was nothing that could be done right now. I gave him my neighbor's phone number and ran back home to console my mom. We were glued to the screen—looking at every survivor, praying that Val's face would appear. We never saw her. I decided my mother should go to Oklahoma City, so I called for the first flight out and took her to the airport. Mom boarded the plane at 1:00 P.M., only to be delayed over two hours due to inclement weather in the area. My mother heard official-looking men aboard the same flight discussing the bombing on their cell phones. She heard them quoting a very high death toll, which made her hurting worse. My mother later told me that the vision of Valerie's face interrupted her constant prayers, saying, "I'm all right, Mom, I'm all right." A kind, older couple sitting with my mom helped her through the waiting by relating the loss of their granddaughter several years earlier.

I drove back to my house, listening to reports on the radio. Tears in my eyes made it difficult to drive. I kept telling myself that they would find her. "Please God, let her come out of this alive." I remembered her smiling face just three days earlier, holding and talking to Taylor. I prayed that God would be with her.

When I got home, I called my brother Greg in Oklahoma City and my sister Michelle in Edmond. We could hardly talk to one another because we couldn't stop crying. I was really not believing what was happening. They still had not found her.

Rhonda's doctor gave special permission for her to travel and my family headed to Oklahoma City Thursday morning. I just had to be there. Surely, I thought, I could do something. I wanted to go downtown and look for her myself. Later I would learn that I couldn't even get near the building. I left Rhonda and the girls at her parent's home in Lindsay, Oklahoma, and drove frantically to my parents' house. When I arrived, we all held each other and grieved while watching reports of the rescue. Many visits to the hospitals proved that none of the unidentified injured matched the description of my sister. Our prayers were for a miracle—that somewhere in all the rubble she would be waiting to be rescued. Hope was still very high. However, it would be nine agonizing days before Val's body was found.

At my folks' house the phone never stopped ringing. There were so many friends and relatives calling to find out if we had any news. We were gifted in so many ways. Their support and kind words were a gift from God. The prayers that were raised for my sister could not be counted. Val had many friends and touched many lives. Her active participation in church and work activities made her a close friend to a great many individuals.

I reminisced about my life with Val. Being a year and a day apart in age, with common interests, brought us very close together. We had great fun growing up together. Our love for sports was the uniting point that would bind us during our short time together. We grew up with a homemade baseball diamond in the backyard. We loved to hit fly balls to each other. And when my friends came over, she was out there playing football or baseball with us. Same way when she had her friends over. We both still played softball, even in our thirties. Valerie and I really grew closer at college. Val was worried about life after high school, so I assured her that she would like it if she came to Saint Gregory's College in Shawnee, Oklahoma, where I was a student. The next year, she quickly became popular. My friends really liked her and accepted her as family. With about three hundred students, Saint Greg's was like a big family, and Val really fit in well. Being close to home made it easier for us, also.

After Saint Greg's, we were at Oklahoma State University in Stillwater, living in a house together for a couple of years that my parents bought for us to use. Val took great care of me. She usually cooked dinner and she frequently did my laundry! We really had a good relationship. Val became one of the biggest OSU Cowboy fans in the state of Oklahoma. She showed it by attending almost every athletic event. I could call her from Texas to learn the latest scores and highlights, and she sent me lots of news clippings. Val was always thinking of me by sending a card or a t-shirt she knew I would like. She was always good to her big brother.

Even as adults, we still would pick a game, an OSU baseball game or football game, and we'd go enjoy it together. She would always look out for me, if she had an extra ticket she'd call me to see if I wanted to go. It was always positive around Val, always upbeat; everything was fun because of her attitude. She always enjoyed what she was doing. After marrying and starting a family, I still got to see Val because she'd take a week's vacation just to come down and be with my kids. My kids loved her. That's what I'll remember always.

I miss my sister and my friend. I miss the relationship she had with her nieces and nephew. The memories we shared are dear to my heart and will always be on my mind. I know she is in a better place now, and one day I will be with her in Heaven. I believe she carried some children from the day care as they rose to be united with our Heavenly Father. I know she is playing with them right now.

I want people to remember Val as someone who didn't have enemies. She was a friend to almost everyone and she was always willing to help someone if they needed it. When

she'd take her vacation to come down and watch my kids—
all on her free time. I also want to remember what a big fan
she was—we'd always get into rivalries. She'd pick a team
and I'd pick a different team, just to have competition.

The fact that Val was there for my daughter's birth and
my other daughter's birthday will always stay with me. If my
daughters hadn't been born that day, Val wouldn't have been
down to see us and I would not have seen her that weekend.
At least Val got to see and hold her new niece, Taylor.

Emotionally and spiritually, Val's death has really affected my life. If it could happen at that place and at that time,
it could happen to anyone. It could happen to you. And if
that doesn't bring you closer to God I don't know what can.
Val made choices about what was important up until her
final day. Although she had no way of knowing the end was
near, she chose to spend her last days with family and friends.
I think it's great the way she got to see all of her immediate
family on the four days before her death.

Our lives will be changed forever because of the thirty-three
years and forty-five days Val spent on this earth. Our family
get-togethers will always have one thing missing, just like the
piece of my heart that left on April 19, 1995.

I love you and will miss you, Peaches. Your big
brother, Terry.

Julie

David Morton
Freshman counselor
Bishop McGuinness Catholic High School
Oklahoma City, Oklahoma

WHEN YOUNG PEOPLE DIE, particularly with the ability Julie possessed, we are the ones that suffer. We suffer not only for the loss of her life, but the loss of the many gifts she would have brought to our community.

Julie was bright, caring, gentle, happy, and not afraid to take risks. She possessed a gift for language, and was able to use that gift by studying in Spain her junior year in high school. Realizing that she would not be able to graduate with her class, Julie accepted the challenge. She enjoyed her wonderful experience abroad and graduated a year behind her class.

My memories of Julie include her often stopping by my office to talk about running, about her year in Spain, or plans for college. Her father, Bud, was faithful about volunteering around school, often helping serve lunch. Bud loves young people, and has often used McGuinness High School students to help at his service station during the school year or the summer months. He would often stop by my office to talk when he was in the building. When he knew that Julie was dead, McGuinness was the first place Bud came. His love for his daughter was evident.

Julie and her family will always hold a special place in my heart. I think about her often and pray that God will continue to heal her family's pain.

Mark Bolte

A) *Mark (second from the left) attending the National Jamboree in A.P. Hill, Virginia. He was a member of Boy Scout Troop 52, Bentonville, Arkansas (1983).* **B)** *18-year-old Mark receives his Eagle Scout medal from Troop Leader Guy Wilkerson. His pastor, Msgr. Murphy, and Joyce and Don Bolte look on (June 17, 1984).*

C) *Mark is elected Knight of the Year by the Knights of the Altar on his Senior year in high school. Mark continued to serve as an altar server at Midnight Mass every year, as was the tradition for Knights of the Altar at his home parish, St. Vincent de Paul in Rogers, Arkansas (April 28, 1985).* **D)** *This group of Bentonville High School graduates, class of 1985, attended school together since Kindergarten. Mark is in the back row, middle. His friend, Mark Porter, stands to his left (with a mustache).*

E) *22-year-old Mark and his younger brother, Matt, at their family's home in Bentonville, Arkansas (1989).*
F) *Graduation day from the University of Arkansas, Fayetteville. Mark is in the center (1990). Mark was an avid Arkansas Razorback fan.*
G) *During his time in Oregon, Mark took advantage of the many natural wonders of the area. Mark (wearing cap) is pictured here with two co-workers at Timberline Ski Lodge, Mt. Hood, Oregon (September 1991).* **H)** *Mark returned to Arkansas to attend brother Matt's Eagle Scout induction (October 1991).*

I) 25-year-old Mark and brother Matt serving at Midnight Mass with Father Richard S. Oswald, St. Vincent de Paul Church, Rogers, Arkansas (1991).

J) *The Bolte family's last portrait together, taken December of 1993, a year and four months before Mark's death. Sitting in front are Don and Joyce. Standing behind them are Matt and Mark.* **K)** *Mark loved outdoor sports. He is pictured here skiing in Colorado.* **L)** *Matt and Mark visit Grandma Bolte in Wisconsin (Summer 1994).* **M)** *Mark plays Christmas carols for the family at the Boltes' home during the holidays (Christmas 1994). He began his new job in Oklahoma City a few weeks later.* **N)** *Mark loved to build and display model airplanes and he received one as a gift his last Christmas. His parents later found this model, unfinished, at his apartment in Oklahoma City.*

O) *Mark's last picture, visiting with his Aunt Retha in Tahlequah. Pictured here with brother Matt (February 1995).* P) *Don, Joyce, and Matt Bolte were greeted upon their return to Arkansas by a display of empathy from their hometown. The Bentonville High School Welcome sign, along with trees in the Boltes' yard and in city parks, had been decorated with ribbons of many colors. The Boltes had been in Oklahoma City two long weeks waiting for Mark's body to be recovered from the rubble.* Q) *Altar servers from St. Vincent de Paul Church in Rogers, Arkansas, flanked the entrance and main aisle to the church as people arrive for the funeral of former Knight of the Altar Mark Bolte (May 1995).* R) *Mark Bolte's casket and display, including the awards and certificates he had earned as a Knight of the Altar Server and Eagle Scout (May 1995).*

S) *In the front of St. Vincent de Paul Church in Rogers, Arkansas, a granite bench has been erected in memory of Mark, courtesy of Joyce Bolte's high school graduating class—Bentonville High School class of 1963.* **T & U)** *Collages of Mark's life which were distributed at his Funeral Mass.*

Chapter 7

Where
there is darkness,
let me sow
light

Mark

Mark Porter, 29
Friend
Data Center Manager
Wal-Mart Home Office
Bentonville, Arkansas

MARK AND I WERE BOY SCOUTS together and we worked together to make Eagle Scouts. We enjoyed the camping, the summer camps, any of the outdoor activities. When we were sixteen, we took a nine-day, 127-mile Boy Scout canoe trip in Canada where Mark and I shared a canoe. When it sprung a leak, we patched it up with duck tape and went on the rest of the trip. We started kindergarten together and we graduated from high school together. Mark and I went to Thomas Jefferson Elementary School and we were the first class in Walton Junior High School, named for Mr. Sam Walton. Bentonville was a small town of four or five thousand people then and we pretty much knew everybody. Even after college we always kept in touch and saw each other when home from school—usually to play basketball. I miss that. My parents were friends with Don and Joyce so I guess you could say we've known each other from diaper age on up.

What do I remember about Mark?

The first thing that comes to mind is that Mark made a good time. Playing basketball was a daily event growing up. I can honestly say that whenever we played basketball I don't think any of us ever saw Mark get aggravated or angry—and if he did, it didn't last for more than thirty seconds. He wouldn't let anyone else get mad, either. Mark was very caring of others and he made sure that nobody got hurt playing. The best thing about it was that he'd always have fun at what he was doing. In fact, he would get into what we called the "giggle zone" and start giggling as he played. The more he made the shots the more he giggled—and no matter how much he giggled he wouldn't miss, no matter where he was on the court. He just kept everybody in a good mood.

When I think of qualities that describe Mark the ones that I think of come straight out of the Boy Scout oath. Mark was brave, clean, and reverent. He made sure he lived by the Boy Scout's oath and motto, always. This was a hard thing to do because we stayed in it through high school. Back then, in the early '80s, being a teenager in the Boy Scouts was not just unpopular, it was something for somebody to pick on you about. We depended on each other. It was hard from time to time for me to make it through the ribbing, but Mark didn't have a problem with it. He persevered no matter what. He stood up for it and believed in it. And if he found someone was being picked on for being in the Boy Scouts or for being in the Knights of the Altar at church, Mark—as big as he was—would just step up and say, "I am, too. What about it?" He just lived that kind of life. Mark stood up for what he believed in, without hesitation.

I think now I have a realization of the loss, but at the same time we all know where he is. With Mark, you didn't have to wonder. You knew he was in heaven. I am not Catholic, but I knew that the Church meant a lot to Mark. I was very involved in my Methodist church, the way Mark was in his. When you're that age, when you're in high school, knowing that Mark was so involved was a witness to me. It was very easy to talk about things like that with Mark. I remember noticing the ribbon on his wall for his Knight of the Year award. That really stood out to me.

Valerie

Gregory M. Koelsch, 37
Brother
Mustang, Oklahoma

GROWING UP VAL AND I fought quite a bit, like most brothers and sisters do. I was three years older than Val, and we went separate ways growing up. We were really on kind of different paths—hers was more of a sports-related curriculum and I'd be at band.

My later memories of Val would be my fondest because she was kind of like a second mom to my little girls. Val was the closest aunt to us in Mustang, Oklahoma, and with her not having kids of her own, she would use her free time to be with the girls. She'd come gather Laurie and Lindsey and just go take them out for the day, play with them. She spent oodles of time with my kids. She'd take the girls swimming at my mom and dad's pool, or she'd go out to the lake with us—just all kinds of stuff. My other sister, Michelle, has lived in Edmond a long time and we didn't get to see her near as much as the girls saw Valerie. In a sense, the girls lost their closest aunt. Fortunately, Michelle has kind of picked up since then.

I miss not having Val at the credit union to answer my questions, to be there to help me with stuff. As a marketing major, Val had a lot of knowledge about marketing strategy and things like that—and she'd give me advice. She was pretty sharp.

Valerie was a real giving person. She seemed to go out of her way to make somebody feel a part of the group, or like they had a friend. She was real big with the youth group up at church, with Young Adult Ministry, and served on the parish council. She just took an interest. Everybody picked up on it. She could make a friend instantly.

I've probably put Val's death behind me the best of anybody, but my family's had a lot of problems with it. My girls, who are six and eight years old, they've really had a hard time with the loss. They still say they miss Aunt Val, and they tell me they still talk to her now.

Julie

Letter from Gerald Felsecker
Executive Director, Society of Saint Vincent de Paul
District Council of Milwaukee
Milwaukee, Wisconsin
to John Mallon, editor of the Sooner Catholic

I WOULD PROBABLY NOT BE CONSIDERED Julie's friend. At least not a close one. I am approximately twice her age. Our lives touched briefly during Julie's freshman year at

Marquette, for about a ten-day period in 1991. During that time, Julie and I had a powerful experience together.

Julie had been a weekly volunteer at the Saint Vincent de Paul Meal Program in Milwaukee. Although I am the director of the Society in this Archdiocese, I never met her in this capacity because the program is overseen by one of our managers. The daily feeding program provides meals to an average of 450 persons per night, drawing many Hispanic families from Milwaukee's South Side. As an adjunct to the actual meal, Saint Vincent de Paul developed a program called Family Friendship for Marquette University students to interact with Hispanic children in a mentoring capacity. The Marquette students are drawn from their campus ministry program and receive no remuneration or class credit. Julie was one of these volunteers whose fluency in Spanish made her come to the attention of the program director.

In January 1991 I had an opportunity to make a second visit to the Saint Vincent de Paul Conference in a little town in the Dominican Republic called Sabana Yegua. The parish in that town is staffed by two Milwaukee archdiocesan priests who saw it as part of their mission to educate Catholics back home about the Church in the Third World. A "Third World Retreat" was offered for those willing to visit the sister parish, live with a poor family, and make a retreat together back in the capital centering on Third World Church issues.

I asked our Young Adult Coordinator whether she knew of a young person who might want to make this retreat and who could also serve as my translator in my dealing with the SVDP conference. Julie was recommended to me. I discussed this possibility with Julie, and she approached her professors at Marquette for permission to be excused from class for two weeks to accompany me. Her logic, which was accepted by Marquette, was that (1) she would be improving her Spanish (her major); (2) she would learn more of the Third World (sociology); and (3) she would learn how Third World Catholics viewed the Church, particularly as a liberating force in their lives (theology).

My impression was that Julie was a quiet yet friendly person with a quick smile and a strong desire to help. I picked Julie up a number of times from her dorm to visit with my wife and me. We took Julie to Mass with us, out for dinner, and introduced her to our friends. My wife and I recall how, on one occasion, Julie was very upset because she had organized a prayer service for peace about the time the Gulf War broke out. It was an outdoor affair, and only a few students showed up. Instead, a number of students had shouted insults down from their dorm windows during the service. This created for me an image of a young woman who was passionately interested in making the world a better place and willing to take unpopular positions for what she believed in. This image was reinforced several times in the course of our subsequent experiences.

Julie and I were two among twenty Milwaukee Catholics who made the Third World Retreat that year. We were assigned to live with families in an outlying village called Las Guanabanas. This was a rough experience for both of us. Although there was electricity in most of the village, there was a lack of drinkable water and the bathroom facilities were primitive. The food was obviously unlike anything we were used to. Even the Spanish was difficult initially for Julie, as the people spoke quickly, had their own pronunciations, and their vocabulary was filled with agricultural references, something Julie had not been exposed to. We bonded quite strongly during those days in Las Guanabanas as we both felt our way. Julie and I were taken under the wing of the local Church leaders who treated us, with their minimal resources, as if we were royalty.

Julie was overwhelmed with her experiences, especially the kindness and sincerity of the people, the physical hardship of life in the Third World, and the power of the faith exhibited by the people. Julie also carried many feelings of guilt: why was life so comfortable for her (as a student) when people were fighting for daily existence? At that point in her life, Julie was trying to reconcile everything she had against the needs of the have-nots of the world. Julie shed tears a number of times as we discussed our "privileged" positions in the world, especially when people approached me through her for help with medical needs, help sending their children to school, etc.

Several of my most precious memories of Julie are very happy ones. One day, after the local people took Julie and me for most of the day on a walk through their dried up tomato and tobacco fields (it had not rained in months), Julie and I returned to the village absolutely dehydrated and dying of thirst. Neither of our houses had refrigeration, so all we had to look forward to was some warm bottled water. We noticed a little shop at the end of town and stepped in to find that they had icy cold *El Presidente,* the local beer, which in our state at the time, tasted better than any beer we ever had before. We quickly downed several bottles and sat and talked with the owner. The owner, by some strange coincidence, had tried to get into American baseball a few years before, and had actually played a season with the minor league team in, of all places, Wisconsin. We couldn't help thinking what a small world it is!

I also remember that, at the end of our stay in Las Guanabanas, the families pooled their money and made something they knew we really would like: macaroni and cheese. This indeed was a treat after eating many things all week that we did not recognize. In Thanksgiving, Julie and I similarly pooled our money to rent a jeep to take the people to the "Disco" in the neighboring town. There they taught Julie their local dances, which she enjoyed immensely, as well as more of their local brew.

At the retreat back in the capital following this experience, I remember Julie in several ways. I recall that her father telephoned her from the States several times at the retreat center, concerned for her safety during the experience. Julie seemed somewhat embarrassed by the calls, although she confided to me that she did have feelings of anxiety and insecurity during the night, and was having difficulty sleeping. I also remember Julie breaking into tears during one of our liturgies as she tried to compose one of the prayers of the faithful. Again, Julie seemed to be having difficulties reconciling what she had in life with what others lacked.

Two weeks after we started, Julie and I went our own ways. We met several more times to give presentations to interested groups using slides we had made from our photos. The next year, Julie went off to Spain and we lost contact with each other. When she returned to Marquette for her last year, we never made contact, although I am told that Julie continued to help out in our meal program.

Julie used me as a personal reference to obtain her job with the Federal Government in Oklahoma a few months before the tragedy.

Chapter 8

*A*nd where
there is sadness,
let me sow

joy

Mark

Joyce A. Gorman, 60
Co-worker, retired
Federal Highway Administration
Austin, Texas

I DO NOT KNOW WHEN I first met Mark, as I lost my husband, Jerry, in June of 1993 after seventeen months of battling cancer—so time is and was a blur to me. After my return to work, I became better acquainted with Mark and asked him if he would be interested in sharing a ride with me. Mark was not a morning person and we had flex time, so it was a real sacrifice for him to agree to share a ride. After thinking about it for a while Mark decided he would give it a try.

While sharing our car trips we became very close friends. Mark listened to me. He also made an effort to share about his life with me. Looking back on our conversations I realize how much he helped me through this time. Mark was a jewel, a rare young man, who reminded me of my son James, who lives in Dallas. In fact, he was like another son to me.

During our riding together I suffered from a lot of headaches so Mark would tell me he would just pick me up so that I wouldn't have to drive, which was out of his way. He even would drive my car for me. He kept on talking even when, because of my headache, I couldn't talk. In his attempts to make me feel better, he also brought tapes to play certain music in the car. Mark loved music and he came from quite a musical family.

In our time in the car we talked of many things. I learned that he had a hobby of model airplanes. I also learned that Mark loved a girl very much but that it had not worked out when he moved to Austin so they were no longer seeing each other. I knew that Mark was hurting a great deal about this.

My daughter and family from Kansas gave me a baby black poodle for Christmas that year. One day I was telling Mark my tale of woe about having never raised a puppy and how hard it was to take care of it. Shortly thereafter Mark asked me if I had an extra minute before getting home and I told him I did. He went into his room and came out with an old sock and said for me to give it to my puppy, Nikki! Mark took the time to be thoughtful in big and small ways. He was just a sweetheart.

While in Austin, he started right away getting active at his new parish and we'd talk about his church and mine. A lot of young people don't do that when they move. At work, Mark was elected to our Federal Highway Administration (FHWA) Social Club and he worked very hard to improve our club. He had a special love for baking cookies and brownies and other gooey things that he would bring into work to share with everyone, and he started up a joint coffee pot to bring us together (before that each work section had their own). Then he arranged our Christmas dance at the Country Club, which became my first social outing since I had lost my husband. Mark worked very hard for the dance and he used his own equipment from home, making it a great success. So I complemented him on the decorations, music, and so on, and then asked him to dance with me. He flatly told me he did not dance, and no matter what I said he would not try! I had not seen this side of him and was surprised. That night, after the dance, he was loading everything up by himself. Finally, after asking several times, he let another co-worker and me help him. He was one of these people that would do anything for anybody. Our FHWA Social Club is—after voting on it—now officially called the Mark Bolte FHWA Club.

Mark showed his love for children in our conversations. He spoke of having worked with them in his church, where his mother played the organ. I knew about his love for playing the guitar and how he and his college roommate used to play and sing. He would bring cassettes for me to listen to that were funny and uplifting. We talked about Christmas traditions while we were growing up. I knew that his mother collected Santa Clauses and I remember how Mark drove down to San Marcos, Texas, trying to find one that she did not have. For his brother, Matt, he would be on the look out for Arkansas Razorback items. Mark was very proud of his father. There was no doubt that he had a wonderful home life.

We had two employees retire and I was in charge of the party. Mark had been to Oklahoma City for a house-hunting trip and had been to Arkansas to see his family. He was back in Austin to pack up his office items and to go to the retirement party. We hugged and said good-bye and I never saw him again.

I was in Kansas at my parents when we heard the news. I had Mark's new phone number and called him. I was so sure he would be out of the office attending a training session. But his father answered the phone and told me that Mark had not been found yet. Although I was not able to attend the services due to illness, I have letters from his parents and a copy of the poem his mother wrote while waiting on his body to be found. I lost two good friends in the Oklahoma City bombing—one a friend for over ten years, and the other, my adopted son of sorts, Mark, whom I loved very much.

Last June in Medjugorje I asked Mary to pray for my loved ones and I know that she is. Mark was a blessing in my life in a very difficult time. I don't worry about Mark anymore. I know that since he was such a good Catholic Christian, as was my husband, that they are angels watching over all of us.

Valerie

Stephanie Palmgren, 33
Friend
Oklahoma Corporate Credit Union
Tulsa, Oklahoma

Before Val and I became friends, we were business colleagues. She was the marketing director for the Federal Employees Credit Union and I was the marketing director for Communication Federal Credit Union. We were close in age, both unmarried, and shared a lot of the same interests in addition to having the same job for two different credit unions. Val's most endearing quality was her laugh. It was infectious.

When Val started laughing everyone started laughing. It was kind of a giggle, really. You know how sometimes people laugh but it's not really a laugh? Val's laugh was always genuine. It made people smile. When I turned thirty, Val mailed me thirty birthday cards—one each day of the month of September. "Do you have any idea how hard it is to find thirty *different* thirty-year-old birthday cards?!?" she laughed.

Val was so very dedicated to her religious beliefs. I was raised Baptist—and because I enjoyed hanging out with her and her church friends, Val always called me a "Catholic-wannabe." Even though I did not know a great deal about the spiritual part of her life, I admired her conviction.

Val was so loved by so many people, and she was kind to everyone. This was evident in everything that she did. Just the other day, I was visiting with a credit union president from Lawton, Oklahoma. Out of the blue, he started talking to me about Val, without knowing that I even knew her. He mentioned that because he was from Lawton, he was somewhat removed from the various credit union circles in Oklahoma. He said that Val always made a point to speak to him and made him feel like a part of the group. Val was a hard worker, dedicated to her job, her career, and to serving her credit union. She was also extremely trustworthy. I could always count on Val. If I shared a secret with her, and asked her not to repeat it, I knew without a doubt that she would not.

The last time I saw Val was the day before she died. She was serving on a marketing committee for the Oklahoma Credit Union League, a trade association for credit unions with offices in the building where I work. Val was scheduled to attend a meeting on April 18 at the League's building in

Tulsa. When she arrived from Oklahoma City, she was angered to find that the meeting had been canceled and she was not notified. She stomped around my office and called some of her colleagues on the committee to see if they had been notified. They had. She ranted and raved for a while, then sat down to visit with me. I had only been on my job for about three weeks, so we talked about how things were going. We then talked about a friend of hers whose nephew had just died of AIDS and how sad it was. We said how very tough it would be to lose a close friend like that. "That would be like me losing you," I told her. We both stopped and thought about this for a few seconds and realized how serious the conversation had gotten. "Why are we talking about such serious stuff," I joked, and we shrugged it off.

Being the dedicated OSU fan that she was, Val wanted to stop by the Cowboy Pete store in Tulsa before heading back. She was looking for a particular kind of Final Four basketball shirt. I decided that I was too busy to go that day, so I gave her directions to the store and we stood up to hug and say good-bye. I noticed that Val hugged me for an extra long time. Not the usual quick hug and good-bye. I remember thinking that she must really miss me, and that I should make more of an effort for us to spend time together.

I remember Val as my best friend. She always provided a shoulder to cry on or an open mind to bounce ideas off. She was generous and kind. She knew more about sports trivia than anyone I ever met. She was a loving aunt. She was crazy about kids. Val talked about meeting the man of her dreams, getting married, and having a baby or two. She was a great softball and tennis player. She was so much fun. We always had a great time no matter what we did.

I have thanked the Lord many times for the precious gift of getting to see Val one last time. I attended Val's funeral with my mother, sister, and friend Christy Sanders from Tulsa. We all rode together and timed it to arrive about twenty minutes before the service began. As we made our way to the church, I noticed that all of the parking spots were taken and the surrounding neighborhood streets were lined with cars. For a moment, I wondered what else was going on in the area. We ended up parking in the neighborhood across the busy main street in front of the church and walking quite a distance. I could not believe how many people had come to the service. I knew Val was popular and loved by many people, but for the first time ever, I realized just how many lives she touched. More than any other time since I had known her, I was very proud to have been her friend, and felt so lucky to have known her and been loved by her.

Julie

Dawn Ribnek, 23
Friend
Newton, Massachusetts

I TRULY HOPE THAT THROUGH MY WORDS many people will see what I have been gifted to know and experience through my friendship with Julie. I think I speak for many of her friends, professors, relatives, and even acquaintances when I say that she was a very special girl, someone who comes into your life like a burning lamp and leaves a deep impression—forever.

Although it's difficult to put into words what Julie means to me, she is a role model in many ways. Her concern for others and her ability to form deep friendships with others was an outstanding quality. Looking back on the days surrounding her funeral, it seemed crazy that fifteen of her friends from all over the country dropped what they were doing (it was the week before final exams for many of us) and drove to Oklahoma. Her parents were astonished, yet, for us, it was the least we could do for such a good friend. Her sincerity and true caring inspired that kind of devotion in the people she touched.

Julie was also an example of heroic struggle in doing the little things of each day—and doing them with a smile. Whether it was homework or a headache or someone who made her wait for them or a problem at home, she went through the inconveniences of daily life cheerfully. I know her parents' divorce was always difficult for her and yet she prayed for her parents and loved them as the best daughter could. Without standing out or doing anything strange, Julie tried to put her faith into practice by praying a little each day, by going to Mass as often as she could, and by going to the sacrament of Confession frequently. I learned that she continued to do this after moving back to Oklahoma and tried to get her parents and friends to do the same. She even went to Mass the morning of the bombing before going to work. I am convinced Julie is in Heaven . . . she can teach us young people not to be afraid to show others a Christian example and to speak to them of God. It is amazing to think that in that short time, God was preparing Julie to meet *Him* a little while later.

I am a pediatric nurse now, working in a pediatrician's office in Newton Centre, Massachusetts. Julie and I met in

October of 1993 in Milwaukee, which was the beginning of her senior year and my junior year at Marquette University, where she studied Spanish and I studied nursing. We met through Petawa Residence, a private intercollegiate residence for students in Milwaukee. I had been living there for two years and I believe her friends at Petawa had a profound impact on her life throughout her last year in Milwaukee, as did the spiritual guidance she received there.

Julie began coming every Friday night to Petawa to a buffet dinner for college students. These nights are a highlight of my college memories, too. Between fifteen to thirty of us from different colleges would gather together, having a great time unwinding from an undoubtedly intense week at school. Julie told us about her year abroad in Spain once at a get-together dinner. She was always able to help everyone feel at home. Petawa did in fact become her "home away from home" in December of 1993 when we became roommates there.

That spring was one of the best semesters I had in college. Looking back, I'm sure it was one of her best ones, too. It was a time of growing up for both of us. She was preparing to graduate and was rediscovering her Catholic faith at the same time, a process full of struggle but a peaceful one, too. Having a firm faith myself, thanks to many good influences in my own life, I tried to help her as best as I could. She once asked me if I knew a good "Morning Offering" prayer and I gave her one that a very good friend had written out for me years before on some beautiful stationery. It was a silly attachment on my part but I gave it to her anyway. After she died I found that very same prayer on her bedside table in her home. She had given the original paper to her fiancee, Eric, but he had returned the favor by giving her a printed card with it in return because he knew how much she liked to say that prayer each morning. The same prayer was also printed on her holy cards at her funeral:

> *O Little Thérèse of the Child Jesus,*
> *please pick for me a rose from*
> *the heavenly gardens and send it*
> *to me as a message of love.*
> *O Little Flower of Jesus, ask God*
> *today to grant the favors I now*
> *place with confidence in your*
> *hands. . . .*
> *St. Thérèse, help me to always believe*
> *as you did, in God's great*
> *love for me, so that I might*
> *imitate your "Little Way" each day.*
> *Amen*

We (all of Julie's closest friends through Marquette and Petawa) had a great time together in her last months at college. She had a great sense of humor, a constant smile and a warmth about her that made you want to open up to her when you needed to. If anyone needed anything—from a ride somewhere to a cup of coffee to help with a paper—she was there. She took piano lessons (something which did not come easy to her but from which we can all learn a lesson in how to struggle!) from an older lady on staff at Petawa, Rose, who became like another grandmother to Julie. I will never forget how Julie searched for the perfect gift for Rose's eightieth birthday and how she gave up several hours of studying time the weekend before finals just so she could help Rose weed the garden.

Our third roommate that semester was Hannah Hach, a student from Kuliacan, Mexico, who was studying English at Marquette. Hannah was also a great friend who kept in touch with Julie through letters until just before Julie died. I also lost my own father to cancer not long before that. The irony is that Hannah was killed in a car accident in Mexico in July of 1995, just three months after Julie died. I am still overwhelmed by those events yet feel incredibly privileged to have lived so closely with both of these women. Humanly speaking, these events so close together could be very devastating. Yet one has to look at it from God's point of view if it is to make any sense. Someone once said, "God is not like a hunter who waits to shoot the little rabbits when they are least aware. Rather, He is like a divine gardener who picks the roses when they are in full bloom."

The last time I saw Julie was May 21, 1994, just before she graduated. I had to go out of town for a few weeks and could not be at her graduation. Through mutual friends we kept in touch after she graduated. I will always remember Julie smiling. I will always remember those incredible days waiting for her body to be found, the fifteen-hour drive to Oklahoma, the strength of her parents during her funeral, and the bond her friends shared—in grief and, yes, even in some ways, in peace. The sight of that wrecked building is still very haunting.

After moving to Boston in September 1995, I asked Julie several times in prayer to help me find a job. She knew how much I loved nursing and, as my roommate, she helped me "survive" nursing school. After several leads and interviews and then weeks of waiting, I got the offer for the job I now have and love on October 19, 1995—exactly six months after she died. Strange coincidence? Probably not.

Chapter 9

O Divine Master,
grant that
I may not so much
seek to be consoled
as to
console

Mark

Letter from Donald J. West
Division Administrator
United States Department of Transportation
Federal Highway Administration
Montpelier, Vermont
to Joyce and Don Bolte

DEAR BOLTE FAMILY,

The Vermont Division office was deeply saddened to receive the final word about Mark. There were a lot of tears in the office on Friday afternoon. Many of us tried to maintain hope that there would be some miracle. We can also understand how important it was to end the waiting.

My wife, Marcia, and I want to pass along our sympathy for your great loss. As you know, Mark was in the Vermont Division Office for over a year. During that time we got to know Mark and to love him. I got to know him best out on the golf course! We have a small division office and we needed another player so that we would have enough players to field a team for the Regional golf tournament. Mark was nice enough to say that he would learn the game to help us out. That is the type of attitude I will always associate with Mark. He jumped right into the game by using my old golf clubs and then buying a set for himself. We spent many an hour at the local driving range. I know they wondered why their business was so good in the weeks before our tournament! Our team spent a lot of time trying to improve our game. Mark was the most conscientious of us all.

We also spent many an hour playing on the West Bolton Golf Course. That is how I will remember him: driving a ball out of sight (boy, could he hit it a long way!) and walking together with him up the fairway. I think this is a male bonding thing that tends to bring people very close in friendship. Mark was, however, a friend to our entire family. Marcia would often say "Why don't you invite Mark over for dinner tonight?" She truly enjoyed his company, as did all of us. He was almost always available to come over to our home and we always had a fun time when he was there.

My youngest daughter, Rebecca, was home from college the summer we came to know Mark. Always wanting to be a part of "the team," Mark joined one of our area engineers on a softball team. Rebecca would frequently go over and watch them play. Becca found Mark to be a wonderful role model and *so* easy to talk to. She even joined us out on the driving range. This was her start of learning the game in earnest. She is now playing frequently with her friends in South Carolina. I know the chance to be with Mark and her dad at the driving range is what gave her the bug. She took the loss of Mark very hard.

I think Marcia recalls most the evening Mark came over to our house shortly before his transfer from Vermont. He insisted on "paying us back" for the hospitality we tried to show him. He asked if he could borrow our kitchen so he could cook a meal *for us*. He brought over all of the food, cooked everything, set the table, and cleaned up afterward. It was a great meal and a great last opportunity to have Mark in our home. It was also the thoughtful, caring, and loving image that Marcia and I will never forget.

I would like you to know how much we loved that young man. His mother and father must have done a great job of raising a thoughtful young gentleman. Our hearts are with you. Mark has been in our prayers constantly since we heard of the bombing. We attended the same church as Mark, where we would see him on Saturday afternoon, sitting on the right-hand side, about half way back. I still look for him there and miss seeing his friendly face. Our parish priest really liked Mark, too. They always had conversations after Mass and you could tell our priest enjoyed them. Our parish has been praying for the bombing victims and we have been keeping Father informed about Mark. I am sure Mark is being prayed for by many people around the country that he has blessed with his friendship. We have no doubt that he is with the Lord.

We all thank you for giving us the opportunity to know Mark and become friends with him. I know these words will not do much to ease the pain you are feeling, but I hope they will let you know how much we care.

Valerie

Harry Koelsch, 61
Father
Oklahoma City, Oklahoma

I HAPPENED TO BE DOWN DRIVING by the Murrah Building within a few minutes after the bombing. Already the officers had secured the area and would not let me go any further than Broadway and Sixth Street. When I looked up and saw the building, still some distance off from where I was—I started shaking so bad that I did not know what to do. I remember thinking to myself "I should go over there, but they're not letting me go . . ."

I went back to the shop and decided that the first thing I needed to do was get a hold of Rosemary in Arlington so that she didn't find out about the blast from the television. I went to my office to try to call her but I couldn't get through. The Oklahoma City lines were jammed—and when I did get through, the Arlington lines were not working. They'd had their own phone problems from a storm the night before.

By then, Michelle, my youngest girl, called me at the shop—and she was hysterical. She just repeated over and over, "Daddy, that's Val's building! Daddy, that was Val's building!" She was crying so bad— and that's when I started losing it. Joe, my boss, was right there with me. He just looked at me and said, "Give me the phone and you go sit down. I'll try to talk to Michelle and calm her down." And he did. He talked to her and got her calmed and he made out that I would go ahead and go up to Edmond to be with her as

soon as we got hold of Rosemary. Soon after that, my son
Terry got through from Arlington and I said, "You better let
Mom stay there because I'm sure Val's going to be in a hospital somewhere and we'll need to know what to do then
and everything." But Rosemary said all the way along that Val
was already gone. That there was no hope that she'd be alive.
I kept up hope for a few days. After we settled when
Rosemary would come back, I went and sat with Michelle
at her place and we waited.

The people from our church, from Saint Pat's—there's just
no words to describe how much they've helped us. That first
day, our friend Agnes Berkenbile stayed with us all day out there
at the First Christian Church as we waited for information, and
then she went down to Saint Anthony's Hospital with us. The
next day Agnes was over at our house first thing in the morning with breakfast. She was hurting so bad, too, because Val had
just been like a daughter to her. And all of Aggie's grandkids
called her Aunt Val. Everyone wanted to help, but they brought
so much food over that we had to tell the priest to please tell
everyone to stop bringing it. It was too much and it was going
to waste. Father Zoeller was really good, and Anne Kirby and all
the people at Saint Pat's. Just anything we wanted, anything we
needed, they were there for us. They were coming to the house
and calling and asking if there was anything they could do. Their
support was just overwhelming. Every bit of that stuff has
helped us a whole lot.

I think I've always had a real strong faith. And I know
it has been strengthened by everything I've seen Val do. Since
then, since she was killed, I knew that relying on my faith
was the only way I was going to get through it. I just don't
know how anybody that doesn't have a strong faith gets

through something like this. My faith gives me so much strength.

It's hard to say all the things I miss about Val. I miss her smile. I miss her calling me at work and how she'd say, "Hi, my Daddy!" Val would always call me up and ask, "Daddy, let's go out to lunch" or "Did you hear about the latest Credit Union gossip?" She always had some little tidbit to share. Rosemary and Val and I did a lot together—and I miss that. We went on several vacations together. Once, we went on one of those all-inclusive things down in an island in the Caribbean. In fact, Rosemary made me a Father's Day gift this year and one of the little pictures she put in it was of Val and me sitting by the pool on that trip in one of those lounge chairs.

Val was such a good Christian person. And she was a good sports person. A story that makes me real proud—and makes me laugh, too—happened when Val was still playing softball in high school. Her team and a whole busload of us parents went to the National Finals in girls softball for that age group. It was down in Texas. We were playing in a game that would take us out of the finals. Valerie played left field. The coaches had always told the girls, "When you get a ball out there you relay it in, you don't try to get it in all the way." But here we are in this tight game, there was a girl on third base and the ball was hit to Val in left field and Val caught it—and Val looked up and she could see that the girl tagged up on third and started for home. So Val threw it—all the way to home plate—and she put that girl out. Everybody just went crazy. Val had saved the game.

Even as an adult Val played on all these coed teams. She was playing on two teams when she was killed. The guys would say "We want Val because we know that she will hit and she won't let them get by us." It's not just all the things she did, you see, but it's how she did them. Val went all the way. When she was involved in something she was really involved in it—just like when she started the Young Adults group at Saint Pat's. She really became involved in that ministry and she even got on the Core Team at the diocesan level. Anything she did, Val gave it her all.

Val was just the apple of my eye. She was quite a little girl.

Julie

Carola Whittet, 57
Friend
United Methodist Church of the Servant
Oklahoma City, Oklahoma

I MET JULIE IN AUGUST OF 1982, when I bought the house next door to her and her mom. Julie's most endearing quality was that she loved all mankind. She wanted to make all the hurts better. I remember Julie thinking of others regarding something that would be important to them. She remembered birthdays and holidays, she had a smile on her face no matter how she felt—and she asked about YOU.

On April 15, 1995, which was Holy Saturday that year, I talked to Julie for the last time. Julie knew that my brother died on an Easter years ago and we talked about how profound and how sad Easter can be. Spring had sprung and we were enjoying it so much. We talked about her future, her boyfriend, her work. I took for granted that I could see her anytime I chose. Our visit was too short.

One of the things that I will always remember about Julie was her pilgrimages to poor countries and poor areas to help the children. She felt so unworthy to have so much after seeing the way many other areas of the world lived. "Things" became unimportant for her and she exuded a maturity way beyond her years. I felt she stood in grace.

I remember Julie saying, "I'll pray for you," and you knew that she meant it. She loved God's nature and tried to protect it. I'll always remember the little girl I first met, and how she grew to be so enjoyable, her musical laugh, her glow. I can't impress enough the goodness that I felt grow in Julie the last two years of her life. I have felt it from people of God before and I felt such love from Julie—for all living things.

Valerie Koelsch

A) *Valerie at age one, flanked by brother Gregory (3 ½ years) on her right and brother Terry (2 years).*
B) *A young Val wearing casts on both feet the summer between her first and second grade.*
C) *High school age Val with younger sister Michele.*
D) *Val loved sports. She played volleyball, softball, and basketball in high school, but her true love was softball. When she played, Valerie remained focused on the game.*

E

F

G

E) *Valerie and a group of friends from St. Gregory's College in Shawnee, Oklahoma, at a dance her freshman year (1980). Valerie is third from the left, standing.*
F) *Graduation day from Oklahoma State University, home of the OSU Cowboys—her team! (May 1984)* **G)** *The Koelschs' last family portrait taken in the early 1980s. Standing left to right: Michele, Terry, Valerie, and Gregory. In front, Rosemary and Harry Koelsch.* **H)** *24-year-old Valerie and brother Terry at their father's 50th birthday party. They were the best of friends.*

H

121

I) *Rosemary, Harry, and Val, all active members of St. Patrick Catholic Church, in a portrait taken for the Church directory in 1990.* **J)** *Val and a group of softball buddies enjoy a laugh together. Val is the first one from the left.* **K)** *Val played on as many softball teams as she could. After her death, her parents found a bag of gloves and bats that she kept in her car at all times.* **L)** *Aunt Val, seen here with Laurie (then 4 years old) and Lindsey (6½) loved to spend time with her nieces and nephew (Summer 1994).*

M) *Val and her Federal Employees Credit Union boss, Florence Rogers, used to dress as a theme in Halloween, wearing costumes to the office. One year they were Lucy and Ethel, another the "Blues Brothers," and another year (pictured here) they were a warden and her prisoner.*

122

N) *Val and her friends (left to right: Kristi Mohr, Kim Whaylen, and Val) from the Archdiocese of Oklahoma City take a break from the action at World Youth Day (Denver 1993).*
O) *Walking into Cherry Hill for Mass at World Youth Day, 1993.* **P)** *Val with niece Kayla, whose 3-year-old birthday party in Arlington Val attended just four days before her death.* **Q)** *Urilla Schachle, Valerie's grandmother, on her 90th birthday. On Sundays, Val loved to pick up Grandma to ride to Church together at St. Patrick's.*

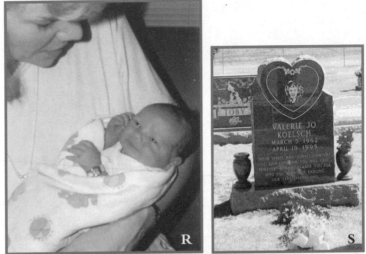

R) *Val's last picture, holding newborn niece Taylor Koelsch who was born on Holy Saturday, four days before the bombing.*
S) *Valerie's tombstone at Immaculate Conception Cemetery.* **T)** *Plaque at St. Patrick's Prayer Garden, dedicated to the memory of Valerie, a council member and long-time parishioner of St. Patrick Catholic Church.* **U)** *Father Ben Zoeller blesses St. Patrick's new Prayer Garden at its dedication ceremony.*

Chapter 10

To be understood as to *understand*

Mark

Matt Bolte, 22
Brother
Bentonville, Arkansas

MARK'S MOST ENDEARING QUALITY was that he thought of other people before he thought of himself. I remember Mark as a big brother who was always there to offer help or advice at almost any time when I needed him to be there. When I was growing up, Mark took me with him to many of the places he went. Most older brothers try hard to get away from their younger siblings but Mark always wanted to spend plenty of time with me. He just dragged me around the world with the rest of his friends. He was usually going to have fun with his own friends, but I'll never forget that he also wanted to take me with him.

I also remember all the fun things that we did. Mark and I both enjoyed much of the same things, like a love for sports. Boy, was he ever an Atlanta Braves fan—from day one! And he loved the Razorbacks. If I went to visit Mark, he would always be sure that there was something fun that the two of us would enjoy doing together—we played golf, we went skiing, or just watched a game. And whenever he would come home to visit, Mark would see to it that we got to spend a good deal of time together. I also remember Mark as a big brother who could be very strict about certain principles and who saw it as his role to help me learn what was right and what was wrong. I very much admired Mark as a person. He set goals for himself and then worked very hard to achieve those goals. It is for this reason that he was as successful as he was.

Mark had a great sense of humor. I remember once how he came and got me and one of my friends and he had us sit and watch him and his friend Mark play basketball. The two Marks would come up to the basket and slam dunk the ball over and over again without missing. They were impressing us big time. We couldn't see it, but they had rigged it so that they had a step to go up to the basket! I also like to tell the story about the time when we were kids that he locked me outside in the snow for an hour and half and laughed at me through the door the entire time! I guess it was a brother thing.

The last time I saw Mark was on Easter weekend in April of 1995. We played golf that weekend, and if I'm right, it was the first time I was able to win a game fair and square.

Valerie

Florence Rogers, 61
President/CEO
Federal Employees Credit Union
Oklahoma City, Oklahoma

MY NAME IS FLORENCE ROGERS, age sixty-one, and I have been the CEO of Federal Employees Credit Union in Oklahoma City for twenty-six years. I met Valerie in late

October of 1984 when I was looking for a part-time marketing director and someone who would also serve me as part-time secretary. Valerie's father, a volunteer director at another credit union, urged her to come visit me for a job because she had just graduated from OSU with a marketing degree. She seemed smart enough and was very personable, so I hired her. Valerie answered my phone and wrote letters and did the newsletter and other marketing for the credit union. We soon became fast friends. Over the years, Valerie became like a daughter to me.

Valerie and I had lunch together almost every day. Other staff members would tease her that she was "brown-nosing" the boss, but it didn't seem to matter to her. During Lent, I could always predict that on Fridays Val would come into my office around lunchtime and say, "Bud, let's go to Captain D's for fish." Even though there was a wide age span between us, Val and I often did things together. We always enjoyed each other's company. Val was always tuned into my moods, as I was with hers, and we both knew when to be quiet and when to have fun. We enjoyed many of the same things, although she was a real sports fan and I am not much for sports. Before coming to work Val always read the sports page in the newspaper. She could keep up with any man when it came to knowing who was who in the sport's arena!

Val religiously sent me cards for Christmas, Easter, birthday, Halloween, and so on, and had gifts for all occasions, especially on Boss's Day. My home is filled with lovely mementos that Val gave me over the years that I will treasure all my life. I have a lovely book that she gave me one Christmas. And every Christmas she gave me a little ornament for my tree, the last one read "My Best Pal." For the past two seasons without Val, the tears have flowed as I put out my Christmas things and find Val's ornaments and the book.

Val's most endearing quality was her bubbly personality and honesty. She was always "up" and seldom moody. I could always count on her to cheer me up if I was experiencing a bad day. She also gave me good advice, even though she had never been married. Her advice was that of an older caring relative. Val was an intelligent young woman. At work, we relied on each other daily to spell words as we were typing different things. And she was always right! She was very meticulous when it came to punctuation and spelling in the Credit Union newsletter.

Val spent many nights in my home and she came to know all of my family. She walked with me through many trying times, including my divorce, and she shared with me the birth of three grandchildren. We shared many sad moments together as we watched my mother slowly die with Alzheimer's disease, finally giving in to the battle in 1989. My mother had been in a nursing home for three years. My family will long remember Valerie. My grandson, now seventeen years old, recently said to me, "Meme, do you remember when Val started up the teen "In-Flight" Club at the credit union? She wanted me to be the first teen to sign up!" Val was always thoughtful that way.

Val loved babies and she got so much pleasure from her little nieces and nephew. In the mornings at work, Val came to my window at the time the little ones in the day care center of the Murrah Building came out to the playground. We would watch them play a while and admire their cute little outfits. Then one of us would end it by saying, "Well, I guess we'd better get back to work."

Val always put everything she had into each project or phase of life she entered into. I remember when she first became interested in country and western music. It wasn't long before she knew about the country stars and purchased their CDs when they first came on the market! On my fiftieth birthday, Val decorated the entire third floor of the Murrah Building. There were huge banners and black balloons everywhere. It was quite a show. She had ordered cake with black decorations and served every Credit Union member who came in that day—over two hundred!

I tried for a long time to talk Val into getting a pet, especially after she moved from an apartment into her little home. She claimed not to like dogs. But she agreed to stay in my home for a week to take care of my little Chihuahua while I was away on a trip. I never did convince her to get a dog of her own.

Many young people could learn a lot from Val. She lived life everyday to the fullest. She enjoyed the simple things in life, such as a day in the park with friends, a ski trip by bus with friends, baseball (her first love), her team spirit. But more importantly, Val was dedicated and loyal to her job. She was respectful of her bosses, and she always gave a day's work for a day's pay. You could depend on her to do what was asked and expected. She learned quickly that dependability was high on my priority list and she never let me down. Val knew she could count on me to let her off early if she needed to leave to take her grandmother to the doctor or on an errand, or to go to Stillwater to her favorite team's games. She gave in so many other ways—and never took advantage of the situation. Throughout her life, Val never strayed far from her religion and beliefs. She loved life and nearly everyone whom she came in contact with.

Val was always so respectful of older people. She loved her grandparents very much and was a real pal to one of her grandmothers. That grandmother made her many lovely things, including a quilt. The quilt was a real masterpiece, and I remember when Val got it how she couldn't wait for me to see it. She was really excited about fixing up her little home, and she was slowly working on it.

The last time I saw Valerie was seconds before her death. I had a meeting of my management staff in my office that started at 8:35 A.M. on the morning of April 19. The meeting was originally scheduled to take place in the board room on the north wall of the Murrah Building. But since my printer wasn't working and I couldn't print out the small agenda, we decided to hold the meeting in my office so that I could read the items right from my computer screen. Val sat in front of my desk, closest to me. The others gathered on chairs and couches in my office. I had taken into work the cruise pictures from my Caribbean vacation to share with everyone. And as people looked over the pictures, one of the vice presidents made the remark, "Hey Ms. CEO, just look around the room at all of the primary colors we have on! We look like a basket of Easter eggs, don't we?" I smiled and looked at each and every one of them carefully. Later, I was able to tell the medical examiner and their families what they were wearing that day as the bodies were being recovered. Val and I owned paisley dresses that were nearly alike and we invariably wore them the same days. We were wearing them that morning.

As I turned around from looking at my computer screen, the entire building blew up, taking all eight of the staff members in my office down six floors and piling tons of debris on top of them. That was the last time I saw those girls. I ended up on the floor of my office, under my credenza, at the edge of the precipice. Where my desk had been moments before there was nothing now. A little triangular piece of floor where I sat and the outside ledge of the wall behind me were all that was left of the office. I escaped by going out the window behind me and was rescued by two General Services Administration (GSA) maintenance employees on the ledge. Once outside, the shock set in and I found myself saying over and over, "My people, my people, I've got to get back in and find my staff." All the people in the room with me perished. None of them made it out. I lost eighteen of our thirty-three staff members that day.

I remember Valerie, first of all, as my best friend. Second, as the daughter I never had. And third, as an excellent employee who required little supervision. Val and I always dressed as some theme on Halloween when we wore costumes to the office. One year we were Lucy and Ethel. Another year we were the warden and the prisoner, another year, the Blues Brothers. She always made me feel as young as she was—and she included me in so many events. Most young people would not have done so, but Val was one of a kind.

When thoughts of Val have surfaced these past two difficult years, I have found myself quickly putting them to the back of my mind. I miss that little gal so much.

Julie

Sara Reed, 28
Co-worker
Social Security
Moore, Oklahoma

JULIE WELCH WAS A GODLY WOMAN who took her relationship with the Lord very seriously. She placed God over everything else, instead of material possessions or money. It is very rare to know someone so devoted.

Julie and I knew each other through our work at the Social Security Administration's Oklahoma City office. I am bilingual in Spanish, as she was. Both of us spent time abroad studying Spanish. We had decided to get together, look at our photographs, and share our memories of these trips abroad, but we never got the chance. That's what I really wish we had had the time to do. I remember Julie's smiling face, her caring personality, and her patience.

Julie's most endearing quality was her ability to accept people for what they were and not to judge them for their mistakes or shortcomings. She exercised this many times with the public at work. I remember once when Julie had a Hispanic claimant with lots of problems. He had even filed once before but had been denied benefits. Julie started that interview about 1:00 P.M. and she stayed with him patiently until 5:00. She took on his new disability claim and walked him through the whole process, showing perfectly that afternoon her ability to accept people, no matter what the situation. She was very patient and kind with this individual and with others that she came in contact with.

The last time I saw Julie was the morning of April 19 when she and I were in the supply room at work together. There were four of us, including Julie, cleaning up the supply room. At 9:00 A.M. Julie told us she had a disability appointment with a Hispanic claimant, and she left us. Two minutes later the bomb exploded. The three of us in the supply room were rescued forty-five minutes later. I'll never forget that look on her face as Julie said to me, "I'll be back in a minute," as she turned and walked away. That image haunts me even now. Sometimes I feel it should have been me that left, not her. I know that's not a very healthy view, but it is my view just the same. She did not deserve what happened to her.

The world lost a caring soul that could have brought the joy of God to others. But maybe now as we all think of her we can look up to her image as an angel and be inspired by what we see. Maybe Julie can bring a bigger path to us from God in death than she could in life. I like to think that about her—and I miss Julie tremendously.

Chapter 11

To be loved as to *love*

Mark

Joyce Bolte, 51
Mother
Bentonville, Arkansas

ONE COMMON BOND
---

by Joyce Bolte, April 30, 1995

Our hearts share the same loss,
Our hurt feels the same as yours.
We know you wonder when peace will come
and will we ever be carefree again.

The one thing you can be assured of
is that we all have one strong common bond:
the day that our loved ones left us
they did not go alone.

They were called by God for a reason,
one that He alone knows.
He must have needed some good engineers
to build new "streets of gold."
God chose us all for a reason,
He knows we trust Him so.
He knew they would do their heavenly work
and still keep watch over us below.

Mark was our first child. He was a joy from the beginning and I loved him with all my heart. I cannot believe some days that he is gone, but then the reality hits again and I am literally torn apart. I will never forget his laugh, his caring ways, his love of life, his faith, and his love for us, his family. Until he got older, Mark always had a big grin on his face in pictures. Then when he got to high school it wasn't a cool thing to do. Mark had a great sense of humor. He had a wonderful, wonderful laugh, and he could laugh at almost anything and make others laugh with him. The most wonderful sound in the world was to hear him laugh. I miss that. I think Mark's most endearing quality was his kindness to others. He always listened to other people's problems and tried to help them.

Mark always loved sports. When he was about four years old he had memorized all the professional football teams and he knew their helmets. I remember going shopping and there was a poster on the wall with all the football teams. The store clerk thought Mark could read because he was sitting on a stool, looking at this poster, and naming off all the teams! Matt, Mark's younger brother, now owns and wears his collection of hockey jerseys. He has all of Mark's furniture, too.

I remember Mark being a joy to be around as he looked forward to a wonderful future. He had finally gotten the position he wanted in his professional life and he was closer to home than he had been since finishing college. That was very important to him. When he went away to college, he didn't feel good about himself for a long time; he had a down period. He could be moody at times and he had a temper but his good points by far outweighed his bad.

Mark loved to send cards to people. He would spend hours in the card shop picking out just the right cards. He would pick out the funniest cards! And he loved to send them to Grandma and to Aunt Retha. He got that from me; I love cards, too. When I look at him in pictures I have to laugh . . . that kid, he never remembered to get a hair cut, never. And he had such thick hair—lots of it!

Christmas was Mark's favorite time of year, and he spent countless hours selecting just the right gift and card for everyone. It was his way of letting people know how special they were. I can hardly bear Christmas now. But for Mark's sake I carry on the traditions that were so important to him and Matt. After all, I still have Matt to love and care for—but the hole in my heart will never heal.

The night of April 19 we received a call from the coordinator at the Federal Highway Administration saying they wanted all the families to go to Oklahoma City, so we left about 11:00 P.M. and arrived in the city the next morning at 3:00. We stayed with relatives the rest of that night and went to the First Christian Church, which served as the information center for the families, the next morning. We were there all day. That evening we went back to Mark's apartment. It was our first time seeing his new place.

When I saw his new blazer sitting there, it hit me so hard. Typical Mark, everything was a mess. The bed wasn't made and the clothes were strung everywhere. For Christmas the year before I had gotten him a big Bible, that's what he asked for, and it was sitting on the coffee table at the apartment. On the table was a model he had started—Mark loved model airplanes, and anything that had to do with his hands, like puzzles. From that day on, every morning we'd go to the First Christian

Church and wait for the medical examiner to come give us an update. And every evening we'd go back to the apartment.

The day after the last person was found alive, Don went up to the medical examiner and asked if there was any chance that Mark was in a pocket somewhere, any chance that he could still be alive—he said no. Later Don asked him, "You don't think that he's down there suffering, do you?" And he assured us that no, Mark was on the fourth floor close to the window and he would never have felt the explosion. That put our minds at ease. The last day before they stopped looking for bodies, they found Mark. Don and I had been really upset because we were afraid the body would never be found. At that point, it was such a relief. From the time we arrived until they found Mark's body, it was absolutely the worst two weeks I ever spent.

Once they recovered Mark's body, I was worried about what kind of shape it was in, so I asked the woman at the funeral home about it. She said, "he's all in one piece." And that eased my mind. I know that may sound silly, but I felt such relief about it. I had heard about people whose loved one was just smashed and about loose body parts that they had to match up. The woman then brought me a little box of Mark's things. It had his class ring with a little dent, his Razorback watch with the face broken, his wallet with all his credit cards, and his Texas driver's license. He had not had a chance to get an Oklahoma one yet—and they found Mark's briefcase, in all that mess. When we opened it up, there wasn't any work in it! Only three decks of playing cards and a bunch of other stuff, but no work!

When we came home to Bentonville, the trees in our yard were decorated with yellow and blue and purple ribbons.

The Boy Scouts had already planted two new trees in our yard in memory of Mark. The sign at the high school was completely covered with ribbons, and there was a tree downtown decorated. The people were so good to us, here, and in Oklahoma City.

Bentonville was always home to Mark, no matter where he lived. I think it's kind of neat in this day and age that my boys have such neat hometown roots. Mark was born here, he went all his years of school here, even when he went away to college and work, anytime he could get home for any of the special events, like Sugar Creek Days, Mark wanted to be here. He was a homebody at heart.

You go on and you have good times. You can be happy for a short period of time, but you're never fully happy. We were a close-knit family and it just completely destroys your life—and you have to rebuild. You don't understand why. And you know you're not supposed to ask why, but you just do.

We've been to the Murrah Building site several times. I love to go down there and look at all the items on the fence. I can do all those things without any problem. Then, all of a sudden, it hits me again—he's never coming back. I miss him. I worry a lot that I'm not good enough of a person to get to be in Heaven with him. I try to remember when Bishop McDonald came to see us after the bombing. He has been so good to us. When I asked him, "How could God have let this happen?" he said, "God didn't let this happen." And he told us, "Just remember that Mark will always be twenty-eight years old and that he will never have to suffer grief and heartaches again." That gives me great comfort.

The last time I saw Mark was on Easter Sunday, a few days before the bombing. The night before Easter, we were all home together and the boys wanted to rent a movie for us to watch. They had both seen *The Lion King* and wanted to rent it for Don and me, so we all watched it. The next morning, on Easter Sunday, Mark was walking all over the house singing "Hakuna Matata." He said, "Mom, do you know what that means? It means no worries!"

Don and Matt ushered at Mass on Easter and Mark sat with me. He left on Sunday afternoon about 3:00 P.M and called about 8:00 P.M. to let us know he had arrived home safely. Mark always did that, he called so we wouldn't worry. I remember saying to him as he left, "We must get to Oklahoma City to see your apartment." Those words will haunt me forever because I did see that apartment all too soon—but Mark was not there.

Valerie

Rosemary Koelsch, 56
Mother
Oklahoma City, Oklahoma

IT WAS JUST A SPLIT SECOND. I could see the outline of her hair and she said to me, "Mom, I'm OK." Here I am, sitting on the Dallas runway and waiting for the plane to take off so that I could get back to Oklahoma City. At first I didn't believe it was really her. I thought I was just starting to see things because I was pretty upset and so worried. Then she appeared once more and said stronger, "Mom! I'm OK." It was as long as a snap. That's when I knew that she was already gone. Someone asked me once when I shared that story if I thought that she was out of the building and in a hospital. But I knew, in my heart, that she was gone.

They found Valerie on the ninth day of searching. We found out later—I didn't want to know this—that Valerie's chest was crushed and her head was crushed, I'm sure from the floors coming down on her. I remember when we went to the funeral home to pick the casket and make all the arrangements, they gave us a little baggy, like a sandwich bag, with her watch, her two bracelets, and one button off her suit. When they opened the bag the whole room began smelling like a dead person . . . and it was all coming off her bracelet and her watch. I was getting nauseated and so I said, "I can't smell this." And so the funeral home said that they'd work on it some more. They took the smell out of it and I have them now. Her round bracelets that she wore all the time were flat on one side and the other side was round. So she was crushed. It helps me to think that she died instantly because I didn't want her to suffer. One night in those nine days that we were waiting—it was raining really hard, and we went to bed about ten, but I couldn't go to sleep. I told Harry, "It really bothers me to lay here in this warm comfortable bed, in these warm sheets, and to know that my daughter is lying in that rain down there . . . in the cold, in that building."

Val's been in two of my dreams very vividly. She was in white, with a kind of beige skirt and white blouse, and real bright each time. One time I just got to talk to her and the other time I got to hug her. When I woke up I was hugging myself. I know that she was letting me hug her good-bye, at least that's how I chose to see it.

When Val was little she had club feet and she had to wear casts for a long time, and then she had to be in corrective shoes. She accepted every bit of that. She never did complain about her ugly shoes or her deformed, scarred feet. She just accepted all of it. When she was seven, at the end of first grade, she had surgery to make her feet a little more straight and a little more narrow so that we wouldn't have so much trouble getting shoes for her. The nurses would give her pain shots in her thighs and you could see the pain on her face. But she wasn't whiny—and she never complained. She was just a really easy child.

My dad was a great punster. He could say things—like a play on words—that could make people laugh. He was real quick with things like that. And I can remember especially at the supper table that he'd have us laughing a lot of times. He also loved baseball so much, and he would listen to it on the radio all the time. Val was three years old when he died, and he thought that she was pretty special. I think Valerie got her sense of humor and love of baseball from my father. Val loved baseball, and she played softball all her life. I started a team after her third-grade year and I called them the "Okies," but the next year those girls knew everything I knew. Val played up until the day she died. She still had a bag with her bats, her glove, and her shoes. I still have it. And I hope someday I can give it to one of the grandkids.

I miss Val's effervescent personality, her big 'ole grin, her exuberance for life. She just did so many things and she was so active. She lived life to the fullest. She did so much for people and was a lot of fun to be with. Val lived out her beliefs—she wasn't phony or shallow. She really lived a good life and she showed that, in her behavior and her way of life. She was a real giving person, a real loving person.

I just wish we could have had her longer. At least she's in Heaven and she's not going through the pain that we are. But I miss her. I'm happy for her that she's with God, but I miss her a lot.

On a weekend retreat for people directly affected by the bombing, Harry and I had a chance to create something, to make something as part of our healing. There were artists there to help us. Harry weaved a basket. He had never done anything like that, ever. And I made a "memory box," using the last things that Val carried in her purse—a restaurant receipt, a credit card, an OSU sticker. Inside I put letters that Val wrote as a child. I named the box "Beautiful Woman."

Julie

Lt. Eric Hilz, 25
Friend
Kelly Air Force Base
San Antonio, Texas

I COULD SAY THAT JULIE WAS MY GIRLFRIEND, but that wouldn't be nearly enough to describe my relationship with her. She was my best friend, the best friend I've ever had to this point in my life.

Julie and I met in August of 1994 at a young adult's prayer group at Tinker Air Force Base in Oklahoma City. I had been stationed at the base ever since early May and had been attending the group every Friday night. On this particular evening, I had just returned from a temporary duty assignment in Pennsylvania. When I first saw Julie, I noticed all the things that usually attract you to someone, like how her blue eyes sparkled and how sweet her smile was. But beyond that, I discovered just how special she was and how much we already shared in common. We were both Catholics and her faith in God was great. It was this combination of beauty and faith that made my attraction to her irresistible. After that night, I didn't see her again for about a month, but she sure stayed on my mind.

I couldn't wait to ask her out. I can't remember ever being as excited about dating as I was about the possibility of going on a date with her. My big chance finally came one night in late September. The prayer group had just finished saying the rosary and we were all standing around in the chapel hallway talking. Julie was there that night and she was just getting ready to leave when I promptly announced out of nowhere that I was going home too. So I followed her outside and she threw a little smile over her shoulder at me, a smile meaning "What are you doing?" more than "Hi there." I found myself asking her where she lived and I was surprised when she actually told me that she lived over near Lake Hefner. I replied that I, too, lived by a lake—but for the life of me I couldn't remember it's name at the time. I just stood there pointing in it's direction and stammering. Julie just stood there smiling and waiting for me to come up with the answer. The name of the lake never came. But we wound up exchanging numbers and had our first date a week and a day later, October 1, 1994.

On our first date, we went to dinner and then to the Oklahoma State Fair and rode the ferris wheel together. My impression of her was that she was one of the sweetest girls I had ever met. Nothing magical or romantic happened on that date, but something special was born. The next month and a half was spent developing the key to any successful relationship—a solid friendship. The inevitable first kiss finally occurred on the Saturday following Thanksgiving. More kisses were shared the very next Saturday when we spent the day at Turner Falls. Something special was growing.

The remaining months of our time together seemed to pull us closer and closer to one another. I suspected that she was someone special the minute I saw her, and dating her did nothing but confirm that. Julie was a very generous person, the kind who would go out of her way to do for others. She possessed a wonderful childlike outlook on life, which made it much easier for her to get along with a "big kid" like myself. We shared with each other our dreams of future roads. I was considering the possibility of getting into creative writing and she wanted to teach Spanish to young children. She was very much in love with the Spanish language and culture, and wanted to use these things to help children understand and appreciate the beauty of all God's people.

Julie's ultimate goal was to learn as many cultures as possible so that she could do the apostolate, or evangelize, to a greater number of people. She knew that religious discussions played only a small role in inspiring others with the faith. She had a sweet nature. She was able to talk to so many people from different walks of life. Her mannerism during all conversations I witnessed were always very kind—just the way she laughed, smiled, listened, and shared the concerns of others. She brought Christ to people by living a life of joy and simplicity in everything she did—her work, her play, her prayers. Julie's rock solid faith was the most unique and endearing thing about her. In the time that I knew her, she simply couldn't do without daily Mass and the amazing opportunity to receive Jesus Christ everyday.

One time when we were in church together, the deacon was making more than just a few announcements following Communion. He just kept going on and on and Julie was vehemently wishing that he'd wrap it up. She didn't want to scurry out of church as fast as she could. She just wanted to spend more time with the Lord she'd received only moments before. The Eucharist was very important to her and she wanted to be on her knees for a time even after Mass had concluded. Her need to devote time to God cut through everything else in moments like these.

Living Christianity as best we could, Julie and I naturally wanted our courtship to be based on Christian morals as well. We were committed to truly caring for each other not just physically, but spiritually and emotionally as well. I feel that Julie would want me to mention that sleeping together before marriage was something that we never even considered. We respected and loved each other too much for that.

One of the most vivid memories I have with Julie took place one morning when she invited me over to her place for breakfast. She always enjoyed playing music during meals whether it be country, jazz, rock, or classical. After we'd finished eating, we were taking the dishes into the kitchen when, all of a sudden, we decided to dance the tango to the selection that was playing. Even though Julie has mastered many dances, I don't think that either of us knew how to do the tango. But that didn't stop us from tangoing all around her living room. When the music stopped, we prevented each other from falling in laughter to the ground by just standing there hugging. That moment was the epitome of our time together. It was joyous. It was innocent. It was supportive.

One evening, I remember I was feeling pretty bad about something that I thought she would think was pretty silly. We were getting ready to say good-bye when she noticed the expression on my face and asked the obvious. At first, I wanted to just blow it off but the concern in her eyes melted me. I started crying and told her what the problem was. She didn't try to trivialize it. She just hugged me and tried to soothe me. She didn't stop until she was sure that I knew she understood how I felt. That was amazing to me. Normally, I wouldn't have cried over this kind of problem in front of someone else but I was so comfortable with her, it came naturally. She seemed to bring it out. She knew how to love others and she knew how to love them well.

Julie and I never made any specific plans for marriage but I think we both believed that it was a strong possibility at some indefinite point in the future. I looked forward to someday proposing to her in her beloved language of Spanish. Of course, Julie never knew about this intention while she lived on earth. But, beyond any shadow of a doubt, she knows it now in Heaven.

Julie made God the center of her life. Giving time to God enriched her work life as well as the time she spent with family and friends. She liked to go out and have a good time like anyone else her age. The only difference was she avoided occasions of sin. I remember our time together as the very definition of youth—romantic, innocent, sometimes wacky, and filled with laughter and with tears.

Julie was not timid. She was not afraid to give her opinion about something. On the other hand, she was just as open to listening as she was to expressing. She was tender and sweet, but also very strong-willed.

Our final date was on my twenty-fourth birthday, April 17, 1995. She gave me a prayer book and took me out to a restaurant called Jamil's and we later shared champagne at my apartment before we kissed good night. We talked on the phone the following night, but that was the last time I saw her.

I realize that God's arms are far better than mine or anyone else's, but I hope that knowing all of my feelings for her will bring yet another smile to her precious soul. Our lives are now on separate roads. She lives forever in Heaven while my life continues upon this earth. I hope to see her again someday along with all the angels and saints. I just thank the Lord that He saw fit to bless my life with someone as rare and as beautiful as she. The joy and spiritual growth that she's brought to me will continue to play a major role in whatever my future now holds.

OUR NEXT KISS

by Eric Hilz

After an evening
Her feet on the step
And I one step below
My lips to her cheek
A kiss we did share

Time would pass
There we stood once more
Much the same as the last
My lips to hers
A kiss we did share

Moments filled with joy
Custom made for two
Her smile was catching
What could be more fitting
Than the kiss we did share?

Days in which we'd struggle
Tough times in the office
In her arms was refuge
As my only comfort
A kiss we did share

In every love lies conflict
My words—sometimes they hurt
Of evasive rings and unsaid things
On a night rare as this we'd repair
With only the kiss we did share

But in love was peace
A peace that comes with trust
A trust that comes with friendship
In all that we did together
Many a kiss we did share

On the day that she left
Eyes spurned tears and arms outstretched
She listened as I cried to Heaven
And her soul to mine
A kiss we did share

When Heaven calls my name
I pray that I will answer
Amidst cherubim and seraphim I'll see her again
In God's own Divine Way
A kiss we will share

Until then Julie Marie.
Love,
Eric Joseph

Chapter 12

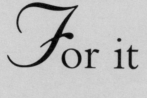 or it
is in
giving
that
we receive

Mark

Dr. Tom Woodruff, 42
Business Marketing Teacher
and Head Baseball Coach
Rogers High School
Rogers, Arkansas

FOR THE PAST TWENTY-THREE YEARS I have served as the altar servers' sponsor at Saint Vincent de Paul Church in Rogers, Arkansas. Mark began serving Mass at Saint Vincent de Paul in the sixth grade and was loyal and dedicated in this responsibility throughout junior high and high school. It wasn't easy for him to make arrangements to serve because his mother, Joyce, played the organ at our Sunday 10:00 A.M. Mass and he served the 8:00 A.M. Mass. Since the Boltes lived in Bentonville, approximately eight miles from Rogers, many times Mark had to stay for the 10:00 A.M. Mass after he had already served.

I especially noticed Mark's "brotherly attitude" toward his younger brother, Matt. It was through Mark's encouragement, good example, and positive influence, that Matt began to also serve Mass. Mark was elected vice president of the

Saint Vincent de Paul altar servers by its eighty-four members for the 1984–85 school year. In the spring of 1985, his senior year, Mark was elected Altar Server of the Year by his peers. Mark's testimony that year read:

> I have many memorable experiences having been in the Knights of the Altar since the sixth grade. The lessons that I have learned will help me throughout my life. Most importantly, however, I have a closer relationship with God and the Catholic Church. It has been a pleasure working with Tom and the Knights of the Altar. I would like to thank them for everything.
> *Mark Bolte*

As Altar Server of the Year, Mark represented Saint Vincent de Paul Knights of the Altar in the "National Knight of the Year Competition." This recognition is based upon the altar server being responsible, loyal, truthful, polite, honest, service-oriented, respectful, and reverent. Mark was the best kind of leader, he led by example and personal actions.

It has become a tradition at Saint Vincent de Paul for former altar servers to serve the Christmas Midnight Mass each year along with the current high school seniors. Mark would always make a point to serve each Christmas when he was in town. The last time I saw Mark was at the Christmas Midnight Mass before he died. I was overcome by a profound sense of sadness and disappointment by Mark's death. Mark was, quite simply, one of God's great people. He never had an unkind word. In his own quiet way, Mark was a winner, hero, and champion.

Valerie

Valerie Mitchell, 25
Friend
Office of Youth and Young Adult Ministry
Archdiocese of Oklahoma City, Oklahoma

I FIRST MET VALERIE WHEN I SERVED on the Archdiocesan
Core Team with her. Her most endearing quality was her
sense of humor. She could always make me laugh or smile,
no matter what kind of mood I was in. Val also had a great
laugh! She had a way of looking at you when you spoke that
said that what you were telling her was the most important
thing in the world. I remember one young adult meeting I
organized in the hall at Saint Eugene's when almost no one
came. I was expressing my frustration over all the work it had
taken to plan it and how everyone said we needed the meetings, but no one bothered to show up. Val just listened to me
and let me vent my frustration. She was good at that.

The last time I saw Val was at the Archdiocesan Youth
Conference on April 1. OSU was in the basketball finals or
something like that, and she was real excited about it. Val led
some of the icebreakers and made the announcements. She
was so energetic and full of mischief—she always had a
sparkle in her eye that said, "You better watch out!" Val
always had a smile on her face and most of the time she was
laughing. She had a great sense of humor and could always
put you at ease and make you smile.

Val made church and Young Adult Ministry a priority
and she stuck to it. In order to go to the National Catholic
Young Adult Ministry Association National Seminar in

Colorado Springs, Val took time off from work and drove down there because she believed in Young Adult Ministry. Whenever I asked her for help she gave it. Val was always willing to sacrifice for her faith. I think she had a lot of fun doing it, but she did make sacrifices to be at the young adult meetings.

I miss her. I miss her smile and her laugh. I miss the notes signed, "the other Valerie." I miss the phone calls. I'm sorry we never had the chance to do the things we talked about doing. I am sorry she was not at my wedding this year. She was always involved, not only at Saint Patrick's but also on the archdiocesan level. Not many single people Val's age would serve on the parish council or be as active as she was. Valerie was a role model in her commitment to her Church.

Julie

Emmett E. "Bud" Welch, 58
Father
Oklahoma City, Oklahoma

JULIE WAS BORN PREMATURELY. She was so tiny and delicate. The first time I saw her, I knew she would be the joy of my life and I looked forward to every minute with her. There is so much I would like people to know about my daughter: the way she seemed to smile out of the side of her mouth, how much she loved to hunt Easter eggs, her love of seafood.

When we went to my mother's house for Easter, Julie would hunt Easter eggs with her cousins—and there were a lot of cousins. Competition for the eggs was pretty stiff. But Julie could find eggs with the best of them. She seemed to have a natural radar. Julie lived with her mother after she and I were divorced and she was not raised with her half-brothers. Family gatherings were especially fun for her because she got to play with so many other children.

When Julie went to Pontevedra, Spain, as a high school exchange student, it was a very difficult time for me. I missed her terribly. I desperately wanted her to come home, but I knew that this would ultimately be a good experience for her. At first Julie was not having a good time. Although she had taken two years of Spanish in high school, she could not carry on much of a conversation. And her host family, the Pintos, spoke very little English. At dinnertime, it was hard to ask, "Please pass the potatoes" when she didn't know how to say it! Spain is where she developed her love of seafood. They lived only ten miles from the ocean and seafood was plentiful. She would send me pictures of family celebrations and the table would be overflowing with lobster, crab, and other delicacies.

I would send Julie care packages of some of her favorite foods that she could not get in Spain, including Kraft macaroni and cheese and Spaghetti O's. She loved Spaghetti O's as a child. It cost me three times as much to ship the package as it was worth, but I didn't care. It was for my little girl.

Sometimes Julie could be difficult. She would call me to complain that she was not allowed to do a particular thing that she wanted to do. The Pintos were very strict, and Julie was very independent. I told her that she had to obey her host family and I would not get in the middle of any problems. But in time she grew to love the family and Spain. That is what induced her to return to Spain in college. While in Spain, Julie studied many languages. Besides speaking fluent

Spanish and English, she could converse in French, Galician, Italian, Portuguese, and German.

Many people from all over the country and the world have sent loving letters telling how much Julie meant to their lives. She cared and tried to make the world a better place. Julie prayed for peace and love among all people, and she demonstrated her concern for world peace by studying different cultures. By studying our differences, she hoped to find the common thread that binds us together.

I want people to remember her kindness, her willingness to help other people, especially poor people. She worried about that all the time. She started her volunteer work in high school when she became a member of the National Honor Society and it was required that they get a certain number of hours of community service. Julie chose to go to the Hispanic Center in Capitol Hill and volunteer there. She was helping people who couldn't read or write either language trying to work out utility payment plans for them. After her official community service hours were over with, she continued doing it. It meant a lot to her.

Years later, Julie's journey to the Dominican Republic as a translator for the Society of Saint Vincent de Paul in Milwaukee was a very moving experience for her. During the three weeks she was there, she lived in the countryside in the barrios with one family. She was shocked that the whole family shared one towel. It was suggested that they take an extra set of linens and leave it behind with their host family. Julie went the extra step and left the linens and towels she was using as well. When Julie got back and told me that they didn't have any electricity or running water, I asked her, "What did you have to do, use an outside toilet?" And she said, "No, Dad, they didn't have those. You used a pan." Julie felt so bad when she came back from the Dominican Republic. She struggled with why they had nothing and she had so much. She really had a tough time understanding the terrible poverty those people have. She was a kind, gentle little girl who cared deeply for people who didn't have the same opportunities she had.

And she turned her experience into a positive thing. She went to work in Milwaukee with Habitat for Humanity helping build houses on Saturdays. I remember one week she called me on a Saturday night and said, "Dad, I'm getting so tired of chopping weeds and picking up tires and automobile parts out of backyards. I wish they'd let me do something else." And I encouraged her to go ahead and do this for a few weeks before asking if they'd let her do something else. She was so enthusiastic. She said, "I want to paint and build some cabinets." But, hell, she didn't know anything about building cabinets! She felt really good when she finally got to paint and even hang some wall paper. Julie got so much satisfaction out of seeing the big smiles and even tears from the families when they were able to move into their own places.

One of the last times Julie drove home from Marquette, I went up to Milwaukee over the July Fourth weekend to make the trek back with her. Here we are in Julie's four-door 1992 red Grand Am getting ready for this long haul home. As soon as we were on the road, Julie pulls a rosary out of her purse. I asked her to wait until we were out of heavy traffic—which she did. And as soon as we were off the interstate highway and on a two lane highway, she pulled that rosary back out! Julie was very devoted to Mary—thanks to her Mom, I think. By the same token, Julie was not one to wear her faith on her sleeve. Her faith was inside her.

Julie's faith influenced me a great deal. After being away from the Church for a long time, I began going to Mass some. I remember when I would be in Milwaukee and we'd be at daily Mass at the Joan of Arc Chapel and, after Mass was over, Julie would stay there and pray for about ten minutes. I'd pray for about three and get up and walk around. I'd wait for her at the back of church. I've thought a lot about my past and I have regret, even guilt, that I abandoned my Church, which I should not have done. But I did it. And I'll never do it again. The Catholic Church is a tower of strength for me today. Julie was bringing me back to the Church before she was killed. She wanted that really bad. And, of course, since her death, I've been going to Mass every Sunday and occasionally to daily Mass. There's no excuse large enough to cause me to miss church on Sundays anymore. I want to go, and I enjoy going. I love my parish, Little Flower.

Julie used to suffer a lot with depression. I learned from Lena, her mother, that Lena would often pray while driving to work, "Lord, let me have the bad day, let Julie have the good day." Lena prayed that prayer the day of the bombing and later said to me that her prayer was answered. Julie went to Heaven while Lena had to live the nightmare of the aftermath. Had it been the other way around, if Lena died and Julie lived, I don't think Julie would have been able to handle it.

Every Wednesday at 11:30 Julie Marie and I would meet for lunch at a Greek restaurant across the street from the Murrah Building. We had a lot of wonderful times, but I always thought that we would have more wonderful times in the future. Now my future will be without her. Julie had met a wonderful Air Force lieutenant named Eric Hilz. There were so many things to look forward to, but now I will never know the joy of walking her down the aisle on her wedding day, I will never hold her children, and I will never again hear her sweet voice saying, "I love you, Daddy."

Sometimes when I go down to the fence, I go to the Survivor Tree. I lean against the trunk, close my eyes, listen to the leaves, and think about the way it used to be. Julie would not want us to be sad. She loved God and now she is with Him in a better place. We must remember the joy of life because that is what she would want of us.

You can kill the body, but you can't kill the soul.

Chapter 13

It is in *pardoning* that we are pardoned

Mark

Calvin Karper, 40
Co-worker
Federal Highway Administration
Oklahoma City, Oklahoma

I KNEW MARK FOR ONLY A FEW MONTHS, but I felt like I knew him better than my own brothers. Mark had just transferred from our Austin, Texas, division office and he was our environmental engineer at the Federal Highway Administration. Being an environmental engineer in our office was not just a job to Mark; he felt very strongly about the environment and he truly wanted to leave this Earth a better place than he found it. He loved his work and he enjoyed the things he did with others.

The person Mark replaced at work was quite controversial and had retired partially because of his frustration with his co-workers. Mark was able to accomplish many of the things his predecessor could not in a very short time because of his ability to respect others and work around their difficulties. I can't find words to describe Mark's most endearing quality. He was a good friend and I miss him a lot.

My wife, Lori, and I looked forward to having Mark to dinner with us because we could talk with him about anything. He would tell us about his family and we could tell that he was very proud of them. In fact, shortly after the bombing we had no paperwork to tell us who to contact. There were no files, no computer records. They were all in the building with Mark. We were able to contact Mark's mother after the bombing because we remembered that Mark told us she worked for Sam Walton at one time. A call to Wal-Mart headquarters in Bentonville was all it took to find her.

Mark was always positive and upbeat. He didn't feel he could reciprocate by having us over for dinner, but when he found out that our son, Barney, was interested in the guitar, he started bringing his guitar over to give Barney lessons. Barney always looked forward to Mark's visits because they had a lot in common. Barney is big for his age and a little clumsy. Apparently, Mark went through a lot of the same things Barney did and he was able to relate to Barney as they visited in the guitar lessons.

When I remember Mark, I see him rollerblading with Barney and me around Lake Hefner, falling down and laughing about it. Then getting back up and doing it all over again. I see him helping my son learn the guitar and joking with him. I see him discussing any subject like he enjoyed talking about it. I see him wanting to learn all he could and happy to pass his knowledge on to others. I see him taking a difficult situation and working out the obstacles through compromise so everyone benefited. That's how I remember Mark. In many ways, I wish I were more like him.

Having a bachelor take time to do things with children is very unusual. But I found out at Mark's funeral that he did a lot of work with teens. They were simple things, like teaching the guitar to my son, yet I know he touched a lot of lives like that. Mark provided a role model for young people, giving his attention to others and trying to leave this world a better place than he found it. He was very certain about his belief in God, his love for Christ, his family. He was one of those rare individuals that truly projects a spiritual presence.

Our son now hangs Mark's guitar, a gift to Barney from Mark's parents, over his bed. It is a constant reminder to him and to us of a wonderful role model and friend. Mark Bolte left this world a better place.

Valerie

The following "autobiography" was written by Valerie when she was twelve years old and a sixth-grade student at Hilldale Elementary in Oklahoma City. For the project, Valerie answered questions such as, "Who am I?" "What can I do?" "What do I believe?" and "How will I spend my future years?"

Already, Valerie's answers reflect the high priority she continued to give to her family and to being the best person that she could be. Her answers are honest, funny, and conscientious.

Yes, Valerie earned an "A" on this assignment from her teacher.

"My Autobiography"
by Valerie Koelsch

MY NAME IS VALERIE JO KOELSCH. I have blonde hair, blue eyes. I weigh 93 pounds and I'm five feet tall. I have short hair and I usually wear pants. I can play the piano pretty good. I've been playing for about one year. I enjoy playing the piano, but I just don't like to practice.

I was born on Monday evening, March 5, 1962, at Saint Anthony's Hospital in Oklahoma City. My mom was glad that I was a girl because she had already had two boys. I'm the next to the youngest of four children. I had a funny incident at age one. While learning to walk by myself, I would always hold my mom's finger when I would walk. Whenever she didn't hold my finger, I would cry.

I play softball for the Raiders. In our pre-season tournament we got second place. We lost the game for First place 7-8. I play relief pitcher and left field.

At school, the subjects I consider most important would be math, English and reading. The most difficult subjects would be science and social studies. The subject I consider most enjoyable is reading.

My purpose in life is to make something of myself, not just be an old bum. My purpose at home is to be helpful and do what's my part of the work. My purpose at school is to learn and not just be there to warm my chair. My purpose in the community is to keep my neighborhood clean and not just go around causing trouble. I hope to carry out these purposes by trying to do everything the best way I can.

What are my wishes? I wish that I could be a better person. To fulfill this wish I try not to lose my temper so fast and not to yell so much. I wish that I could be a real good pitcher. And to fulfill this wish I'm practicing really good and hard.

I believe that my friends should be truthful and honest. I believe that school should teach me things that I don't know about but want to learn about. I believe that in work every one should do his or her share. I believe that everyone should go to church. I believe that with the way the government is going now, somebody should get in there and change it.

My favorite adults are my aunts and uncles, Grandpa and Grandma, Mom and Dad, and a whole bunch of other people. When you come into my house you can smell cooking and scented candles. My favorite room would probably be the living room. It has gold carpet and a big picture window. My favorite piece of furniture would have to be the divan. My dad uses it the most. I like it because it's soft and you can stretch out on it.

I think it's fun being one of several children, because you can divide the work instead of having to do it all by yourself. Also, you have someone to play with and you learn to share. I think that the happiness and love in the family is made by everyone. I think our family friends are good to have because you have different people to play games with and talk to.

Some of the games that our family plays are: scrabble, softball, basketball, tennis, badminton. We enjoy barbecues, going to the lake, and going on vacation. Everybody in the family likes to read. Mostly, everybody differs in what they read. What my family wants most out of life is peace, joy, love, and happiness. I think my family fears most a tornado, a fire, a theft, or a death in the family.

What does my family believe about life?

Life is what you make of it. We try to stress the good or positive side in a life situation. We believe you receive in measure what you put into something. My family expects me to act good.

I really don't know when I first discovered my emotions. They were happy emotions, though. When my emotions are harmful I try not to show them. They're helpful when they cheer someone up. When I experienced my greatest emotion of fear was during the tornado a couple of years ago. My mom helped me overcome my fear. During this ball game, I came home and the ump called me out, but I was safe by a mile. I just held my anger inside. When Mom and Dad came back from their trip my emotion was love.

I'm going to spend the future years caring for my family. I plan to spend my future years in Oklahoma City. I'd like to live in a house. I expect that some of the responsibilities I'd have would be taking care of children and other things a wife and mother does. The kind of person I'd like to spend the future with is a person who is funny, happy, loving, active, and a person who is not a grouch. I don't think I owe the government anything but I need to be a good citizen.

A good life cannot be built without dreams. On the job I'm going to work hard. In society, I'm going to be a good citizen. To reach the goals of my dream I'm going to be a good person and do the best that I can.

Julie

Rev. John Michalicka
Church of Saint Mary
Ponca City, Oklahoma

JULIE WELCH WAS LIVING WITH HER MOTHER and attending McGuinness High School while I was pastor at Epiphany of the Lord Catholic Church, Oklahoma City. I regret to recall that during her high school years she experienced apathy and was a victim of peer pressure. This social pressure meant that you belonged to the "right group of friends" and you had the "right clothing." These things were important and regular Sunday Mass attendance was not. Those years of high school were a struggle for her. But perhaps out of this came her beautiful spirituality a little later.

Julie became an exchange student to Pontevedra, Spain, during her junior year. Julie was starting to search seriously about the purpose of life prior to that, and she was starting to choose more "Catholic-like" friends, but the focus still wasn't clear. Julie wrote to me from Pontevedra, sharing that she was enjoying her new family, a good year, and some wonderful Spanish customs. Apparently, the more structured Spanish customs were good for her.

She came back to Oklahoma City and retook her junior year in high school. Julie began to make changes in her life. She made wonderful grades, even receiving a scholarship to Marquette University. During these college years her spiritual life and spiritual growth seemed to be in the "Express Lane." At Marquette, Julie found some contradictions in the life of some collegians who claimed to be Catholic but lived an un-Christian life. I recall using the parable of the chaff and wheat to explain the challenges of living in a community. She began to take her faith seriously. And she sought out and found those who lived up to their Catholic commitment. I think as she sorted this out, these challenges deepened her faith and increased her personal love for doing God's will.

Recollections that I treasure most about Julie are her early struggles in high school years and her willingness to visit about them later; her spiritual development in her last year of high school and beginning of college when her commitment to the Catholic way of life became real; her discovery of personal prayer and a new growth of learning to trust; her faithfulness to Sunday Mass; her love for the Eucharist, frequent daily Mass, and the sacrament of reconciliation; her smile, her gentleness; her sensitivity to others and to her conscience.

Julie Welch

A

B

A) *8-year-old Julie with her father Bud at her uncle's wedding. In spite of her parent's divorce, Julie worked at having a special relationship with each of her parents.* **B)** *Lena Welch with her only child, Julie Marie, on graduation day from Bishop McGuinness High School in Oklahoma City (1990). Julie was a member of the National Honor Society at Bishop McGuinness.* **C)** *The summer before her Sophomore year at Marquette, Julie traveled to Alaska for two weeks with friend Beth McGuire, who took this picture of Julie after they climbed*

C

D

to the top of Deer Mountain in Ketchikan, Alaska. "Neither of us had really done that before," McGuire remembers. "It was amazing."

D) *As a sophomore in college Julie went back to Spain for one semester, attending the Marquette in Madrid Program. Her mother Lena visited her there. In this photo Julie (first from left) and her mom enjoy dinner out with some friends. Until her death, Julie remained in touch with many of the friends she made while living in Spain.*

E) *Julie traveling in Spain.* **F)** *Julie had a special relationship with Our Lady. During her travels in Spain and Europe, she loved to visit shrines and collect special gifts to share with family and friends.* **G)** *Julie's friend and fellow Marquette student, Erin Wright, prepared a special birthday cake in honor of Julie's 19th birthday.* **H)** *20-year-old Julie (second from left) with Gerald Felsecker, Executive Director of Milwaukee's Society of St. Vincent de Paul, and friends during their trip to the Dominican Republic.* **I)** *Christmas Day 1992. Julie visits with her grandmother, Dortha Welch, at her father Bud's house.*

173

J) *A few friends from Petawa Residence, an intercollegiate residence for women in Milwaukee (March 1994). (Julie at bottom, right.)*
K) *"Walk Like an Egyptian" during snack time at Petawa Residence (March 1994). (Left to right: Sarah Hollingshead, Yoly Noriega, Angelina Mateega, Hanna Hach [deceased 7/95], and Julie)* **L)** *Julie and her parents, Lena and Bud, on graduation day from Marquette University, Milwaukee (May 1994).* **M)** *Julie and friends on graduation day. Standing next to Julie is her friend Sharon Hefferan.*

174

N) *Julie and her boyfriend, Lt. Eric Hilz* O) *Julie hands out Halloween candy to the Murrah Building day care children. Julie loved children, and she visited with the kids as often as she could.* P) *Easter weekend 1995. Julie, her mom, and her boyfriend Eric went to visit the azalea gardens near Julie's grandmother's house in Muskogee, Oklahoma.* Q) *Julie's last photo. On Easter Sunday, Julie and her mom Lena enjoy a visit on Grandma Compassi's swing in Muskogee, Oklahoma—just three days before the bombing.*

R) *Julie's friends from Milwaukee and Marquette University who attended her funeral, April 1995. Photo taken at the home of Bud Welch (in front, center).*
S) *Memorial at Little Flower Church in Oklahoma City. The words are engraved on a piece of marble from the Alfred P. Murrah Building remains.*
T) *A spontaneous memorial for Julie is attached to the chain link fence surrounding the remains of the Alfred P. Murrah Building at the bombing site.*
U) *23-year-old Julie Marie Welch.*

Chapter 14

*A*nd it is
in dying
that we are
born to
eternal life

Mark

Donnie Moore
Family friend
Memorial Dedication: April 19, 1996
Saint Vincent de Paul Catholic Church
Rogers, Arkansas

ALONG WITH MANY OTHERS here at Saint Vincent de Paul Church, I watched Mark Bolte grow up from a little boy with red hair and freckles to the big 6' 4", 250-pound man he became. *Man* is a strange term to me when I think and talk of him. I always thought of him as a boy, but of course *man* is the proper term. Mark was a man. And he will forever be twenty-eight years old.

He was an Eagle Scout. He was an altar server and a Knight of the Year. He was a typical boy growing up here in Bentonville, not much different from many of the youth here today. He was a Garfield fan, a Razorback fan, a sports nut, and he liked model airplanes. I watched as he worked his way through college dreaming of being an aeronautical engineer and deciding later to become an engineer in the environmental field.

There was nothing pretentious about Mark. He did not assume the world owed him anything and he knew he had to work for everything. Quite a stark contrast to the persons responsible for his death and the deaths of the other 168 souls in the Oklahoma City bombing. Mark was a very polite young man, highly thought of in his job at the Federal Highway Administration not only by his peers but the local community. He had been in Oklahoma City a short time, but he was already making a difference. He was a gentle person and a "giver"—not a "taker." He would always give his time and talents to others.

There was nothing phony about Mark Bolte. I remember how he would come home every year at Christmas and serve at Midnight Mass. He always had a kind word for everyone. Even as a single young man, in all his travels around the country, he found time every year to send Christmas cards to family and friends, something I find as being unusual.

When I look around for role models for young people, I think of Mark Bolte. I am sad to think that a lot of you will be deprived of the opportunity to be associated with him. He wasn't a highly visible person—a movie star or in the NBA or the NFL or a rock 'n roll singer in music videos. He was an American who worked hard to get what he wanted and lived by the rules. He was a real person with hopes and dreams like all of us and he never forgot where he came from. He retained the values given to him by his parents and this Church.

When his parents were staying in his apartment in Oklahoma City while they searched for Mark's body, they discovered his well-worn Bible. It was obvious he had been reading it frequently. They were surprised at the extent of Mark's faith. The priest with them at the time said they need not worry about Mark, he knew where he was headed someday and was prepared for whatever the outcome of the search was to be. Mark's favorite saying was from a song in *The Lion King* movie, "Hakuna Matata"—it means no worries. Mark is now at peace and has no worries.

On behalf of my family and many others I want to thank the friends of the Bolte family for this memorial bench and thank the church for allowing it to be placed here—on the front lawn of Saint Vincent de Paul Catholic Church. This is a fitting location for it not only for Mark, but for his family (Don, Joyce, and Matt) and his church family and the community. This white marble bench reminds us to abhor violence and practice peace, love, and forgiveness. Whenever we pass by this memorial it will remind us that every time we part from family and friends to begin our daily activities, none of us knows when that last hug, kiss, or good-bye will be. It reminds us to make the most of those moments.

Valerie

Rev. Ben Zoeller
Homily at Mass of Christian Burial: May 1, 1995
Saint Patrick's Catholic Church
Oklahoma City, Oklahoma

MIDDLE OF LAST WEEK, when I was praying for Valerie and for you, a phrase from one of the early Church Fathers that was very popular on posters during the 60s and 70s came to mind. It says "The glory of God is a person fully alive." And we all know, as you wrote in the obituary, that Valerie was so filled with life that she lived as much in those few short years as most people do in a couple of lifetimes. Through her baptism, Jesus Christ, using His divine power, came down from heaven and embraced her. He adopted her, giving her divine life for the very first time. But you know and you believe as she did, that Jesus does not just give us this divine life and then leave us. Jesus gave us His Body and Blood. Again we believe that the bread and wine are not just drama, externals, simply signs that remind us of some historical event. We believe that gathered here at this altar Jesus once again uses His divine power. He comes thundering down from His Heaven to change those common food and drink, bread and wine, into His own Body and Blood.

And so, with this divine life—with His own Body and Blood—that Valerie received on March 18, 1962, He nourished Valerie week after week throughout her life. And we saw how she was able to integrate her human life and her divine life in a very, very wonderful way. The same excitement and enthusiasm with which she played softball she had even that much more excitement and zeal for the trip to see the Pope in Denver. Her enthusiasm could hardly be contained as I went to bless them as they were on their buses. She was just bubbling over with excitement. And how close she was for the opening ceremony when the Pope went by—just fifty feet away. She had that kind of zeal for her faith but it wasn't just in these great huge events.

So often Valerie would go and pick up Urilla and bring her here to Saint Patrick's, her parish Church, to celebrate. And it wasn't with an attitude of "Oh, my, I have to go pick up Grandma." No, you could tell the excitement, the joy that was in her eyes to be able to do something like that. A new parishioner told me that when they came to the parish just about a year or so ago, that Valerie, from the very first moment, remembered their name. That's kind of important to people to have somebody remember your name. But she was that kind of person.

As I said, she brought joy and delight to all of us—by serving on the parish council during a very difficult time, seeing the importance of being together, to create community, to make a family happen, not just in word but in deed. When we did not have Young Adults here at Saint Patrick's she was still involved with the archdiocesan office and other parish Young Adult groups. Her faith was that strong. She didn't say, "Saint Patrick's doesn't have one so I don't need to get involved." She didn't have that attitude. She went the distance to make it happen.

She lived that LIFE! And she gave life! And now, we believe that she has life even more abundantly. She lived that combination of human and divine life here. And she also gave that to her family, her friends, her Church, her work. We believe that when she died, Jesus Christ her Brother, her Lord and Savior, came down from heaven one more time, not to judge her, not to condemn her for whatever faults and failings someone might have. But rather, to take her by the hand and bring her to the throne of Almighty God and say "Father, here is my sister." And she at that moment begins to share the fullness of life. And that is what we celebrate today. And in celebrating her life and in remembering her life, we have one more thing to do. Each and every one of us must commit ourselves to be filled with life, better than we did yesterday or last week. Make a commitment to live our life to the fullest, to integrate that human life and divine life, and make a difference in your parish, in your home, in your work—in everything that you do. So that one day when we have to approach this final passage from life through death to eternal life, that our family and friends will also rejoice and be comforted in knowing the strength of our faith, that bedrock foundation that nothing, nothing can shake.

Right now we need to commit ourselves to be very tender and gentle and loving people. Because of who Valerie was, she left a very large hole in who we are and that is filled only by our love and care for each other. And so, as we make the commitment to live with that fullness of divine life, let us also commit ourselves to comfort one another with even greater love.

Julie

The following are a series of three articles, two by Sooner Catholic *editor John Mallon and the other by columnist Kathleen Howley written shortly after Julie's death, reflecting on her life.*

"Good-bye, Julie"

Editorial (May 7, 1995)
***The* Sooner Catholic**
newspaper of the Archdiocese of Oklahoma City
by John Mallon, editor

I DIDN'T KNOW JULIE, I just felt like I did. She was one of those people I felt like I knew even though I'd never met her. I was even at the point of asking her if she went to the same university that I did, so familiar did she look.

She was young and pretty, yes, and as a single guy I notice those things. But that wasn't the issue, there was more. It was as though God had shone a gentle spotlight on her. I only ever saw her at Mass in my parish, Epiphany of the Lord, in Oklahoma City. She seemed to be one of Jesus' special friends. She stayed after Mass each week to pray—really pray. Clearly she was a friend of Jesus. I like to know people who are friends of Jesus. I want to be friends with them. I fully expected that one day I would have a chance to properly initiate a conversation with her. Still, I didn't know her name.

Last weekend I noticed she wasn't at Mass. Then Father Stieferman announced what he said many other preachers in Oklahoma City would have to say in church that Sunday— that we'd lost a parishioner. He said her name was Julie Welch, 23 years old. I was trying to place a face with that name, and the face of this girl whose name I didn't know came to mind.

After Mass I asked Father Stieferman who Julie was, and he said she was a daily communicant and very devout. I said, "Not the one who used to sit over there"—and I motioned— "and pray after Mass . . . ?"

"Yes."

"Oh, no."

Julie worked in the Federal Building.

Then I recognized some people from the young adult prayer group that meets at Tinker Air Force Base on Friday nights—that great group I keep promising to visit and write an article about. Julie was a member, and her friends had come to Mass at her parish to honor her.

Her body had been recovered, they told me, and the thought of her delicate, petite frame covered, bent and broken under concrete and rubble horrified me. She was not made for that. The image could not have been more out of place.

But I also couldn't help thinking she must have had a real straight shot into heaven. She *was* made for heaven, and *that* image fit, albeit much too soon for my thinking. But after all her visits with Jesus, which I discreetly observed after Mass, I knew that when she saw Jesus face to face they would need no introduction.

But Julie, I am still looking forward to *our* introduction.

Till then,

The friend you never met,

John

"Hello, Julie"

Column (May 21, 1995)
***The* Sooner Catholic**
newspaper of the Archdiocese of Oklahoma City
by John Mallon, editor

THIS COLUMN IS CALLED "For the Real World" based on a notion that C. S. Lewis frequently explores. Namely, that this life on earth is merely the Shadow-Lands, and that the land of reality, light, clarity and substance is the life to come—Heaven. Lewis says in the Great Divorce, "Heaven is not a state of mind. Heaven is reality itself. All that is fully real is

Heavenly." Saint Paul says in First Corinthians, "For now we see through a glass darkly, but then we shall see face to face and know as we are known."

In the last issue of the *Sooner Catholic* I wrote an editorial called "Good bye, Julie," about Julie Welch, a fellow parishioner at Epiphany parish, whose prayer life I admired, and whom I hoped to meet one of these Sundays. But Julie was taken from us before that Sunday came. Or was she? Or is she just with us now more than ever? Christianity says yes. Of course we mourn and grieve, and rightly—even necessarily—so. But I have been astounded by the number of people Julie has touched even in death. God must have put her right to work.

My editorial was picked up off the wire service and reprinted by a surprising number of Catholic papers across the nation. I have been getting calls, notes, e-mail messages, and faxes from people all over the country about her. A striking example is the article reprinted (below) by Kathleen Howley. Kathleen is a syndicated columnist in the Catholic press based in Boston, who first started appearing just around the time I left that area. We had never met. By chance one day last week I came across her e-mail address. The same day I faxed my editorial about Julie to the *Pilot* in Boston. My friend, Father Joe O'Brien of the *Pilot* staff, immediately faxed back Kathleen's article which they were printing; amazed at the coincidence. Kathleen had not seen mine.

I e-mailed Kathleen, introduced myself and expressed amazement at how much she knew and how much she was touched by Julie, whom she had never met. I heard from Julie's college roommate. People were being touched and it all had a delightful Communion-of-Saints-feel to it. I heard Julie had volunteered at Little Flower Parish helping with Spanish translation, and thought by now Julie must be fast friends with the Little Flower herself, St. Thérèse of Lisieux, who was just about the same age as Julie and a great friend of Jesus. Then a friend who knew Julie told me she had a great devotion to St. Thérèse. I am not canonizing Julie, but all this only stands to reason for someone who lived the sacraments and prayer as intensely as she did. Julie's parents graciously came to see me and I had tears tingling in my eyes and goose bumps.

What am I getting at? Simply this: I said I liked befriending friends of Jesus. I have since met friends of His who are friends of Julie's. I said I had hoped to meet Julie. Saint Paul tells us so beautifully, "Faith is the substance of things hoped for." In this life—the Shadow-Lands—we should—and do—miss Julie. We weep, we hurt, we mourn, and it is right that we do. Jesus wept, after all, just before He raised Lazarus. Perhaps He was weeping over the fact of death happening to His friend. But our faith tells us that she, and all our beloved dead, are still with us in a very real—the most real—way. I closed my editorial telling Julie I was still looking forward to being introduced to her. I just didn't realize it would be so soon. Blessed be God.

"A God-Centered Life"
by Kathleen Howley

ON THE LAST NIGHT OF HER LIFE, Julie Welch, 23, probably didn't realize the full meaning of the words, "Holy Mary, Mother of God, pray for us sinners, now and at the hour of our death." She had recited that phrase hundreds of times. She didn't know that her hour was at hand.

Julie had plans for the future. She was preparing to quit her job as a claims agent for the Social Security department to take a job teaching Spanish at a local high school.

She was young and attractive. And, she was in love with a handsome, 24-year-old second lieutenant from a nearby Air Force base named Eric Hilz. They had talked about marriage, but that was still in the future. There was plenty of time—they thought.

The two had met at a Catholic prayer group for young adults at Tinker Air Force Base. Last fall, on their first date, they went to the State Fair and rode the Ferris wheel.

On their final date, the Monday night before the Oklahoma City bombing, they went to dinner to celebrate Eric's 24th birthday. Julie gave him a prayer book, and they shared a bottle of champagne. The last time Eric saw her, after kissing her good night, she seemed very happy, he said.

Julie attended Mass every day, and went to Confession every week. She had a habit of praying the rosary each evening, before going to bed.

She hadn't always been as ardent about her faith. Her father said she was lonely at college, and became depressed after living alone for the first time. That's when she started working on her relationship with God, praying daily, and frequenting the Sacraments. After graduation, she lost 40 pounds, and told her dad that she felt not only spiritually but physically fit.

The morning of the Oklahoma City bombing, Julie attended the 7 A.M. Mass at Saint Charles, as always, before going to work at the Federal Building.

By 9 A.M., she was at her desk chatting with her supervisor. At 9:01 she put down her glasses and went into the front office to greet her first customer of the day—a Hispanic man who needed a disability check.

One minute later, the Social Security office was gone, demolished by a madman's bomb. About half of the 38 employees made it out alive, but not Julie.

"She was too young," said her supervisor, Lorrie McNiven, who woke up in darkness 30 minutes after the blast and was able to crawl from the twisted rubble to safety.

Julie's parents got a call from the coroner's office on Saturday morning. Their daughter's body had been identified. The grieving family said they considered themselves fortunate, because at least they can bury their child. Authorities say that some bodies were obliterated in the blast, and may never be recovered.

To the world, Julie's life was unusual. Daily Mass, the rosary, and weekly Confessions. She was happy, and at peace. It's not something the secular press can easily explain.

At a time when the concept of womanhood has been redefined by the likes of *Cosmopolitan* magazine to mean self-centeredness and self-fulfillment, Julie was a contradiction.

She kept her life God-centered, and wrapped herself in the Sacraments. She had her eyes on the ultimate prize: eternal happiness in heaven.

"We know there is no doubt her soul is in great shape. I feel a real sense of peace. I know everything is all right," said her boyfriend Eric.

Most people will find that statement to be a bit puzzling. To them, death is the ultimate defeat. Everything ends at the grave. Happiness depends on whether we have what we want in this life. But, to a believing Christian, death is only a beginning and earthly happiness doesn't compare to the bliss of spending eternity with God.

That's what Julie showed us, with her life. The body is fragile, and can be blown apart by the act of the murderer. But the soul is immortal, and can't be harmed by earthly dangers.

Its fate, for better or for worse, rests in our own hands.

© 1995 Kathleen Howley

PART THREE

Toward
Healing

Chapter 15

*O*nly
in
God

For the past year, I have collected information about three young adults who died April 19, 1995, victims of a horrible act of violence. My hope and prayer has been—as I collected interviews, letters, poems, personal essays—that I be able to put the faith of Mark, Valerie, and Julie into life-giving words. It has been a task of faith, a task of love, a task of humility. The people who chose to share the stories of their friends, their siblings, and their children, have opened themselves in simple giftedness to the rest of the world. Their honesty has been our reward. And their grief is now shared by all who read their story.

PRAYER FOR THE VICTIMS

by Lt. Eric Hilz
(from Tinker Air Force Base Prayer Service)

She was someone's daughter
A little princess
Whose every step her parents watched
Delighting them with her smile sweet
Lord, take her precious soul gently into Your arms

He was someone's son
The little man of the house
His life so filled
With wonder, discovery, and love
Father in Heaven, keep him now as your own

She was someone's sister
All secrets safe with her
Growing up together
Step by step, side by side
Lord, may she rest with you forever

He was someone's brother
In him, others placed their trust
Offering love and support
He was always there
Lord, in Your kingdom, prepare for him a special place

She was someone's mother
There to nurture a life
Raising a child, a difficult task
She paved the way to peace and prosperity
Reward her, almighty God, for her patience as Your child

He was someone's father
His child he protected
With a heart full of love and dedication
He offered it all for his family
Oh Lord, be his strength and salvation

She was someone's wife
His one and only
The joy her presence brought to him
Hers was a friendship for life
Holy Spirit, may her soul exult in You

He was someone's husband
Her prince and her strength
To her, he gave his life
All to win her love
Lord, hold Your champion forever by Your side

They were someone special
That all of us have known
Many a soul they touched
In their time upon this earth
Heavenly Father, be their everlasting breath of life

Amen.

The bulk of the work for this project has taken place at the same time that the Church remembers and celebrates the centenary year of the death of Saint Thérèse of Lisieux, including the conferring of the title "Doctor of the Church." And, if it's true that coincidences are God's way of remaining anonymous, it's hard to miss God's hand in the parallels found between Saint Thérèse's life and the youthful lives and young deaths of Mark, Valerie, and Julie. In a very real way, Saint Thérèse offers the model by which we remember them. Like Saint Thérèse, these three young adults chose to live the "little ways" of love in their everyday lives.

One Faith

LOOKING OVER THE STORIES of Mark, Valerie, and Julie, it is obvious that they had much more in common than simply the building where they worked and where they died.

Mark, Valerie, and Julie shared a passion for life. And they expressed their love of life by being people who chose to smile and laugh—and who did so often. Over and over their friends and family described them as people who enjoyed life, and who enjoyed the fun things in life, like playing and watching sports. Mark enjoyed basketball, golf, and had started to learn to rollerblade. Julie loved biking. And Valerie played softball on every and any team she could join.

They were the kind of people who enjoyed sharing their deep appreciation for life with those they loved, and often did it in writing. As a result, Mark, Valerie, and Julie left behind many cards, letters, and poems that tell their family and friends how special they are. This zest for life was also evident in their openness to learn, to grow, to explore new ideas, to undertake new challenges, and to experience the unknown—no matter how unfamiliar. Mark learned how to golf when his co-workers at his new job assignment in Vermont said they needed one more player for their team. Julie took up learning the piano as a college senior, taking lessons from an octogenarian. And Valerie became a leader in Young Adult Ministry when there was a need in her church, a ministry totally unfamiliar to a marketing major. All three young people lived a childlike joy in their day-to-day lives. They enjoyed laughing. They appreciated the small things in each day and were thankful for them. And they had a deep respect and recognition for nature as a special part of God's creation.

The stories of Mark, Valerie, and Julie continually confirm the deep gratitude and respect that each of them had for their grandparents, for aunts and uncles, and for the previous generations in general. In stark contrast to contemporary society's castaway elderly, the older generations in the Bolte, Koelsch, and Welch families were respected and enjoyed by both parents and their children. And Mark, Valerie, and Julie showed their strong devotion, admiration and commitment in their choices. Valerie witnessed to many as she frequently took her grandmother to Church on Sundays. Mark was known for taking the time to visit his grandmother, even several states away—and he regularly took out-of-the-way detours to visit his Tahlequah, Oklahoma, family on his travels to and from Bentonville. Julie verified her commitment to family by consciously choosing to return to Oklahoma City following graduation to be closer to her grandparents and parents. She loved to take time with her extended family on weekends and holidays, and she did so often.

Mark, Valerie, and Julie had genuine, strong relationships with each of their own parents. They made time to get to know their mother and father as adults, as people of faith, and their choices reflected that interest. It was not unusual for Mark to go home to Bentonville to spend time with his parents, Don and Joyce—to go to church together, to ask his parents' advice in shopping for a new car, to go to church functions, even to "hang out" with them watching a movie. Valerie, who attended Saint Patrick's Church with her parents, often participated in church activities with Rosemary and Harry. And the Koelsch's have many fond memories of trips and vacations that Valerie planned and made with them as an adult. For Julie, working out time with her parents was not a chore but a joy. In addition to living with her mother after returning to Oklahoma City from Marquette, Julie frequently attended daily Mass and went walking after work with Lena. She loved to stop by her father's service station just to visit, and she had a standing date to meet Bud for lunch every Wednesday. If a child's relationship with his or her parents is any kind of reflection of their spiritual relationship with their Creator, Mark, Valerie, and Julie had an intimate and familiar understanding of their God.

Without a doubt, the most important thing that Mark Allen Bolte, Valerie Jo Koelsch, and Julie Marie Welch had in common was their profound and authentic Catholic faith. Their lives are examples of believers who not only professed their faith, but who lived it daily in the common and ordinary aspects of their lives. None of them had careers that were directly connected to what we know as ministry. But they brought their faith to life not only in what they did, but in how they did it—how responsibly they performed in their jobs; how they treated the people they had to serve; how they related to and respected their co-workers. Like Thérèse of Lisieux, Mark, Valerie, and Julie reflected in how they lived their lives that they, too, were friends of Jesus.

Not only were all three active participants in their parishes, it was obvious to those who saw them—both because of their Sunday and daily presence at Mass and because of their devotion—that these three young adults had a personal relationship with Our Lord. In addition to being open to sharing his talents, like teaching guitar to a co-worker's young son, Mark was devoted to the Boy Scouts and to Knights of the Altar, activities that promoted core Christian values and moral traditions, providing a model for younger people, including his own brother, Matt. During and after college, Julie was very active in social justice issues, publicly praying for peace, visiting with young Hispanics in Milwaukee and Oklahoma City, and helping build shelters for the homeless. And during her last year of life Julie became involved in a weekly prayer meeting at Tinker Air Force Base, where she met her special friend, Eric Hilz. In addition to truly befriending the people who entered her life, Valerie was involved both in the parish and archdiocesan level in promoting and leading Young Adult Ministry—even to the point of considering leaving her job at the Credit Union that she so loved in order to pursue the ministry full-time.

Like Saint Thérèse, Mark, Valerie, and Julie discovered in their own faith life that God did not require from them great deeds, only love. They chose to respond to God's invitation by following a life of prayer, service, and love. And they did so within the regular, everyday, even ordinary situations of their personal and professional lives.

We Remember

FOR MONTHS FOLLOWING THE BOMBING, Oklahoma City was flooded with letters, cards, donations, and gifts from people all over the country. The Archdiocesan Department of Catholic Education alone received over fifty thousand letters, homemade cards, and pictures. Thousands of others were sent directly to the two Catholic high schools and seventeen elementary schools throughout the archdiocese and to parish youth groups—all conveying, as best as words can, the sympathy and love of believers across the nation.

The most moving, perhaps, were the simple words of children across the nation writing to children in the Oklahoma City area:

> Dᴇᴀʀ Oᴋʟᴀʜᴏᴍᴀ Cɪᴛʏ,
> I am sorry and I wish I could take the pain away but I cannot. Our hearts go out to you. I am very sorry about the disaster. I am with you and so is God,
> *Caroline*

> If you need someone to talk to, call me or write to me at . . .
> *Lindsey*

> Even though I don't know you, we still care.
> Sincerely, *Justine*

> I was crying because it hurt. I am sorry,
> *Carrie*

> Dear students at Saint James, the fourth grade class at Annunciation Church will be preparing the Mass next Sunday. We'll offer our Mass in honor of all the children who were affected.
> Love and peace,
> *Taul, Kaylee, and the rest of the class*

> I'm sorry about the bomb! This guy is sad (sad face) :-(
> With love and care,
> *Beth*

And when the national wave of love subsided, the local churches persevered. The Bolte, Koelsch, and Welch families all tell the same story of appreciation for the consistent care shown by their own parish families. From the first few days—when the needs of each family were of the practical and physical type, to today—when only prayers and hugs can help. The families know they have gained comfort, healing, and strength in their journey from the unending support of their home parishes: Saint Patrick Catholic Church, Oklahoma City (Harry and Rosemary Koelsch); Church of the Epiphany of the Lord, Oklahoma City (Lena Welch); Little Flower Church, Oklahoma City (Bud Welch); and Saint Vincent de Paul Church in Rogers, Arkansas (Don and Joyce Bolte, and their son, Matt).

"I'll never forget all the people taking care of us while we were in Oklahoma City," remembers Don Bolte. For Don, Joyce, and Matt, Oklahoma City became their home away from home as the family waited for over two weeks for recovery efforts to find Mark's body. And in the compassion of the people in Oklahoma City the Boltes found a new family of faith to call home. "They would bring food, they would visit with us, they treated us as friends," Bolte recalls. And at First Christian Church, the Red Cross center for families, "lines of people would bring things to distribute to us everyday."

Bolte will also forever remember the giving response of an entire city to rescue workers at the site. "One morning they said they needed heavy leather gloves," Bolte notes, "but by the afternoon some glove company had sent them an entire trailer load of gloves. The giving, the caring, was so impressive. There were a lot of people pitching in to help."

Over time, many memorials of various kinds have been erected in the memory of those who died on April 19, 1995. Some were organized for individuals, some by cities directly affected by the bombing, some by organizations of those who knew the victims, and some were dedicated by individual federal agencies to those employees who died.

"All the things that have been done for Mark, in his memory, have really helped with the healing," says Joyce Bolte. According to Bolte, as recent as this spring she was notified of a new memorial for Mark. "The last project that Mark worked on in Texas was the schematics for a bridge somewhere by Amarillo—and they're going to dedicate that bridge to Mark. There will be a marker with his name, an explanation of what happened, and my poem on it," Bolte explains.

Other types of memorials for Mark have included scholarships funds at his high school in Bentonville and in Rogers, Arkansas; a Bentonville city park marker; a Boy Scout memorial; books donated to the high school library in his name; a grove of trees planted in Virginia; a bronze plaque at each state's Highway Welcome Center for Mark and the other Federal Highway employees killed; and a granite memorial bench erected in front of Saint Vincent de Paul Church in Rogers, courtesy of the Bentonville High School Class of 1963, Joyce Bolte's graduating class.

At the University of Arkansas, the Arkansas Academy of Civil Engineering has placed a "distinguished past member" plaque in the student study lounge in honor of Mark and fellow Arkansas graduate Ronota Woodbrige, who also died in the bombing. Although Academy members are usually twenty-year alumni who are elected on the basis of an outstanding career, the Academy representative said in a letter to the Boltes, "I believe that one day both Mark and Ronota would have been members of the Academy."

"Things like these have meant a lot," Joyce Bolte adds. "To know that people thought enough of Mark to do things like that for him. And, of course, time itself has brought healing, as well as the trial being over."

Rosemary Koelsch knows that her belief that Valerie is with God has brought peace in the middle of their suffering. As has taking on the challenge of forgiving the perpetrator of this act.

At first, Koelsch remembers, "We went to everything they had available for the families of those who died—and that was all therapeutic in itself. Every time we went to something we retold parts of the story. We cried again. We prayed again. And we healed a little more."

The Koelschs attended a lot of tree plantings and memorial services, such as the one at Putnam City Mayfield Middle School, where Valerie attended. And the different memorials made them aware that "we're all united in our grief and in our loss. We found comfort in that unity."

At Saint Patrick's in Oklahoma City, a Memorial Prayer Garden was built and dedicated by the Parish Council to the memory of Valerie, a fellow council member and long-time parishioner. At the ceremony, attended by more than fifty members of Valerie's extended family, Father Ben Zoeller blessed the new cross in the garden, praying that "we who look upon Christ crucified should re-commit ourselves to be a people of faith, a people of love, and every day take whatever cross the Lord places upon us and follow Him—

doing in return what He did for us to begin with." A bronze plaque attached to the marker is engraved with the words: "Saint Patrick's Prayer Garden dedicated in memory of Valerie Jo Koelsch and the victims of the Oklahoma City Bombing, April 19, 1995."

The Koelschs have found great comfort in knowing their parish family was walking with them every step of the way. "There is great caring and sense of 'family' at Saint Pat's," Rosemary notes. As a continuing reminder of their caring, the parish composed and compiled poems, photos, and letters written to Harry and Rosemary and in Valerie's memory. The collection of personal messages was presented to the Koelschs in a formal album.

A POEM FOR VALERIE

by Bob Fritz
Saint Patrick Catholic Church

She was the beautiful sunset on a fall day,
The fragrant meadow in spring.
She was the power of a summer storm,
The pure white snow of winter.
This seasonal woman is now gone,
But her presence is still felt.
For she will never truly leave us,
Just listen and you will hear her.
Only her physical essence is gone,
Her spirit lives on in our minds and hearts.

Dear Rosemary, Harry, and family,

Richard, Dick, and I want you to know how much we miss seeing Valerie's cheerful, wonderful smile at Sunday Mass. She was always so cheerful and thoughtful of others. It has always been a pleasure seeing her with Urilla and knowing how much she cared for her. I often thought how sweet it was to see her bring her to church and to be at her side.

The last time I saw Valerie was at Stations of the Cross during Lent, when she led the Young Adults into church carrying the cross. That was a special night I shall always remember as a lasting memory of beautiful Valerie. I know she has a special place in Heaven. Those of us who have known her since she was a child, know there is no one any kinder or sweeter than Valerie.

Your friend,
Marilyn Smith
Saint Patrick Catholic Church

Other memorial's for Valerie have included a scholarship fund in her name set up by the Sheet Metal Workers International Association as a reminder of "the dangers that all workers face on the job site, whether construction workers, production workers, or office workers." In the Bricktown downtown area in Oklahoma City, historic bricks were placed near the flagpole with the names of each of the twenty Federal Employees Credit Union employees and volunteers who died at the bombing.

"We're not healed yet," Rosemary Koelsch remarks. "I don't know that we'll ever be, but at least we don't obsess as much. At first I thought of Val day and night, I could never quit. I cried every day and it would get a little better. Then someone said to me, 'Well, at least now you're completing your sentences. At first your voice would trail off and you would just quit talking.' But you know, we didn't even know we did that."

For Harry Koelsch, being able to talk about his daughter's death with co-workers, with people at their parish, and with other family members has been the most helpful. Harry and Rosemary also agreed to be part of the Murrah Memorial Committee organized through the Mayor's office. "The best thing that I got out of the committee was seeing the people affected by this be able to come and pull together," Harry Koelsch says.

But perhaps nothing has helped him as much, he adds, as "people coming up and just giving me a hug." On the other hand, Koelsch adds, he found it difficult to handle people that came up to him and declared, "I know what you're going through."

"Unless they've lost a child to something like this, they have no idea what I was going through," he explains. "I have a good friend who lost a son in an auto accident and he's told me: 'Harry, when my son was killed it was bad and it's still bad. But we didn't have it brought up everyday, we didn't see it on the TV and the newspaper. Once it was done it was over with.' And he's right. This is a whole different thing."

Lena Welch notes that, although she stayed away from many official events during the first year, she has recently become friends with several family members who lost a loved one at the Murrah Building. "I met many of them attending the closed circuit telecast of the trial," she says, "and that really helped me. We exchanged our feelings and we cried together. I know these people understand my hurt."

Over the past two years, there have also been many memorials in Julie's name. The organization with which Julie traveled to Spain in her junior year of high school, Youth for Understanding, established a fund in Julie's name that will "enable recipients to learn, through Julie's legacy, that respect for cultural differences and an openness to learning from others are essential foundations for world peace." And her high school graduating class, the 1990 class of Bishop McGuinness High School, raised money to purchase a religious article in her name for the new school chapel.

The Church of the Epiphany of the Lord, Julie and Lena's home parish, will dedicate a new classroom being built to Julie, placing a picture of her with an explanation of her life and death. And at Little Flower Catholic Church, a church dear to Julie's heart, a fountain was built next to the statue of Saint Thérèse of Lisieux. At the edge of the fountain, next to the rose bushes surrounding Saint Thérèse, there is a piece of granite from the Murrah Building with the words: "In memory of Julie Welch and all the victims of the April 19, 1995, Oklahoma City bombing," along with a quote from Saint John of the Cross, whom Julie admired,

> *"Que bien sé yo la fuente que mana y corre*
> *Aunque es de noche"*
> (For I know well the spring that flows and runs,
> Although it is night)

Perhaps what has brought Lena Welch the most comfort, however, has been the certainty that Julie is in Heaven. "God was absolutely first in her life, over Eric, over Mom and Dad, over her work—nothing got in Julie's way. How could I not be happy for Julie?" she pauses. "Even though I really do miss her, I feel her presence often in my life. I know she's with me. I want to be in Heaven with Julie some day, and I want to do the right things so that I will be there. That strengthens my faith."

"I think the thing that has brought me some healing and has even been a vent for some of my anger is the drive to continually tell people about my Julie Marie," Bud Welch says. "I want the whole world to know who this kid was. Why I have such a desire to do that, I don't know."

Welch jokes that, while Julie was alive she would get angry if she found out her father was bragging on her or her accomplishments. Now he can get away with it. "She would absolutely not tolerate that when she was around!" he says.

For the past two years, Bud Welch has been very available to the local and national media, offering his perspective on everything from the tragedy, the plans for a Memorial, even his opinion on the trial and the death penalty. "I just have a real desire for people to know who this kid was. That's real important to me. And for me, the media has been the vehicle to do that."

Welch frequently talks with people at the downtown site, which he visits regularly.

"I go down there about twice a week and I enjoy talking to the people who come and visit because I'm honored that they do that," Welch explains. "A lot of times strangers will come up to me and ask questions like, 'Where was the front door to the building?' or 'Where was the truck parked?' And I'll show them. It gives me an opportunity to tell them who I am and tell them about Julie."

His visits with those who journey daily to the unforgettable site have become a form of ministry for both him

and the visitors from around the world whom he has encountered. "These strangers will share their deepest thoughts with
me. It's a very positive thing—to touch and see and talk and
visit," Welch says. "I don't know how many people I've had
cry on my shoulder just through our conversation."

Like Bud Welch, Joyce Bolte agrees that talking
has been a source of healing—including in television and
newspaper interviews. "We've always talked at home about
Mark and the things that happened. We had so much fun
with him. And those are things you want to remember. For
me, talking is a part of the healing process."

Bolte has also made it part of her ministry to reach out
in writing to people she hears about who are suffering from
the loss of a loved one—whether she knows them or not.
Like the letter she wrote to each family of the TWA plane
disaster. For her, writing letters is a direct way of reminding
those who suffer that "there are many people praying for you
and asking God to help you through this most devastating
time in your life."

Only in God

IT WAS, QUITE LITERALLY, a split second of destruction.

When the two-ton bomb exploded on April 19, 1995,
a spraying wave of steel, chrome, and glass showered north on
downtown's NW Fifth Street. Experts say that in seven-
thousandths of a second the shock wave slammed into the
building, putting nearly a half-ton of pressure on every
square inch of the building's surface. The wave lifted all nine
floors, snapping the two-inch steel bars in the concrete sup-

port columns and causing them to crumble. Three of the building's main support columns were destroyed.

The rapid rise and fall of the floors crushed everything below. And as the blast wave dissipated, the floors collapsed.

In a tenth of a second it was done.

It has been more than two years since the devastating bombing. And the damage that the split second of destruction left behind has been impossible to ignore. For the hundreds of people who were directly affected by the tragedy, either as survivors or as family who were left behind, life will never be the same. They have learned to go on, they have learned to persevere. But they will never forget.

When asked what they would say to someone who is grieving the loss of a loved one, the Bolte, Koelsch, and Welch families all agree in the same first step. Begin by turning to God.

"Try to get God in your life. Try to open yourself up," Bud Welch emphasizes. "Let Jesus help you. I truly believe that He will, but you need to show the effort and desire. How else is He going to be able to help if we keep slamming the door on Him?"

Joyce Bolte agrees.

"You have to believe in God. You have to believe that you'll see your loved one again someday," says Bolte. "And then you have to go on. Someone along the way gave me a Helen Steiner Rice poem called 'When I Must Leave You' that says:

> *And for my sake and in my name*
> *Live on and do all things the same.*

I try to remember that every day."

Rosemary and Harry Koelsch believe that an important part of healing is to let yourself give, to do something that involves ministering to other people. "I would first begin with prayer," Rosemary Koelsch explains. "Take some quiet time to listen to God. He will lead you in the direction of action. Harry and I find a lot of support in the emotional energy of singing. So we are going to take up a ministry to sing a lot of the old gospel favorites at nursing homes."

Joyce Bolte also believes that it is important to find the delicate balance between the extremes of pretending a loved one did not exist and making a memorial of your home. "I don't want to sit around and grieve for the rest of my life," she explains. "The important thing is to keep them alive in your family and in your thoughts. And I ask Mark to help me because I believe that he can," she smiles. "And I know that it will always be hard. There's a special place that Mark left that nobody will ever fill."

Ultimately, Bolte adds, "The only advice you can give is that you have to live one day at a time. And to trust in your faith. Some days you won't find something good—it's there, but you just can't see it. But it helps to look for that something good in every day."

While time eases the pain, only God can heal the broken heart.

"Knowing that Mark is in Heaven, and that he's happy helps," Bolte declares. "The fact that I'm not worried where he is—and the belief that we'll see him again someday."

Lena Welch points out that often what is unsaid is what helps the most. She recalls the time a co-worker came to see her at her desk right after she returned to work. "He stood there," she remembers, "and he simply said, 'Lena, I don't know what to say.' I smiled at him and said, 'you've said it all.' You really don't need to say a lot of words to someone who is hurting. You just need to be there to listen, to try to understand the moods, the cycles that the person goes through. And if I did say something, I'd tell them to have faith. They will see their loved one someday."

For Bud Welch, who still carries in his wallet a little piece of paper cut out into a heart that Julie made as a kid, it is the telling of the stories that will enable Julie Marie's faith to remain a gift. "I get a warm feeling when I get the chance to talk about who my Julie Marie was."

This collection of stories is not a chronicle of how three young people died in the Oklahoma City bombing. It is a testament of their faith, and of how they lived the humble virtues of ordinary life. In order to present who Mark, Valerie, and Julie really were, I have allowed the voices of those who knew them best to tell the stories of their lives, to simply "talk about them," as Bud Welch would say. I pray that these stories will bless you as they have been a blessing to me. With the voice of Saint Thérèse of Lisieux, along with Mark Allen Bolte of Bentonville, Valerie Jo Koelsch of Oklahoma City, and Julie Marie Welch of Oklahoma City,

let us go forward in peace,
our eyes upon heaven,
the only one goal of our labors.

A

B

C

A) *Bud Welch was one of a dozen Oklahomans who visited with President William Clinton at the White House, presenting him with the approved plans for the soon-to-be-built Oklahoma City bombing Memorial (August 1997).* **B)** *This memorial will be run by the National Park System. The monument will consist of 168 empty stone chairs facing a reflecting pool and the American elm (Survivor Tree) that withstood the impact of the bomb.* **C)** *Memorial to be built by Archdiocese of Oklahoma City on the grounds of St. Joseph Old Cathedral across the street from the Murrah site.*

Afterword

By Oklahoma Governor Frank Keating and First Lady Cathy Keating

LIKE ALL OF OUR FELLOW OKLAHOMANS, we were stunned by the magnitude of the Oklahoma City bombing. During the long days and nights that followed April 19, 1995, as the death toll continued to climb, we had the privilege of meeting and getting to know many of the families who awaited word of their loved ones. We were struck by two things: the faith and courage displayed by those who waited, and the profound quality of those 168 lives we had lost. The victims of the bomb were distinct individuals, many of them young people of tremendous potential. They were our neighbors. We are all poorer for their loss.

Time after time, as we learned the stories of those who fell victim to the bomb, we grieved those losses in the knowledge that they left awful gaps in our society. Those who died were volunteers, parents, responsible and caring citizens, members of churches . . . the foundation of a healthy society. Thanks to Archbishop Eusebius Beltran and author María Ruiz Scaperlanda, you have had an opportunity to meet three of them whose faith and lives were so wholly intertwined that we can only wonder at what they might have accomplished had they been allowed to live.

Julie Welch was just twenty-three, a Spanish translator in the Social Security office. She often attended Mass at a local Hispanic parish, and hoped to be a Spanish teacher. After the bomb, her mother Lena recalled that Julie's favorite song as a child had been "You Are My Sunshine." Julie brought sunshine and a living faith to so many.

Mark Bolte was twenty-eight. He worked in the Federal Highway Administration and helped lead a Scout troop. He had been an altar boy, and he carried a strong, active faith with him into adulthood.

Valerie Koelsch, at thirty-three, was already marketing director at the Federal Employees Credit Union. She was a Eucharistic minister in her parish, where she also helped found the Young Adult Ministry and served on the parish council.

Julie, Mark, and Valerie were people of faith. They lived that faith—in their parishes, at work, in their relations with others.

Had these three young people been allotted the biblical three-score and ten, they would have given nearly 130 more years to humanity. They would have enriched our world in incalculable ways. They would have strengthened their parish homes and made their communities happier, healthier, better places for all of us.

That's what might have been. This book is about what was—and what is.

The legacy Julie, Mark, and Valerie left us—like the legacies of so many other victims of the bomb—should serve as a challenge. If in their relatively brief lives these three young people contributed so much, what can we do to fulfill their prayers? What is their true memorial?

The answer emerged in the first days after the bombing. Rarely in American history has a community come together in faith as Oklahoma did during April and May of 1995. Those who came to us from other states—the rescuers, the media, the volunteers—were amazed at our courage and our togetherness. If a job needed doing, it got done. If supplies were required they appeared. When the grieving and the wounded sought solace, it was provided. Our churches were filled, and so were our hearts.

From one act of evil came a hundred thousand acts of love. That is the legacy of Julie and Mark and Valerie and all the others. By their living example they taught us the power of faith. That faith sustained us through a terrible ordeal, but it also reminded us that trust in God is not just a matter for the difficult times, but one for each day, each hour, each moment of a well-lived life. The bombing did not create an atmosphere where goodness emerged; it tapped a deep existing reservoir of that goodness. We were reminded that as exemplary as their living faith was, Julie Welch and Mark Bolte and Valerie Koelsch were three among many. There were others to pick up their banners.

May we all be inspired by these three exemplary lives, and may we remember their families in our prayers. It has been a humbling privilege to know them all.